Leading from the Lockers
Student Edition

John C. Maxwell
Leadership Books for Students
(Based on *Developing the Leader Within You*)

Leading from the Lockers:
Student Edition

ISBN 0-8499-7722-3

Leading from the Lockers:
Guided Journal

ISBN 0-8499-7723-1

The PowerPak Series

Leading Your Sports Team

ISBN 0-8499-7725-8

Leading in Your Youth Group

ISBN 0-8499-7726-6

Leading at School

ISBN 0-8499-7724-X

Leading As a Friend

ISBN 0-8499-7727-4

"These books are outstanding. John Maxwell's leadership principles have been communicated in a way that any student can understand and practice. Take them and go make a difference in your world."

—DR. TIM ELMORE,
Vice President of Leadership Development, EQUIP;
Author of *Nurturing the Leader in Your Child*

Leading from the Lockers
Student Edition

by
John C. Maxwell
with
Jean Fischer

Tommy nelson
Thomas Nelson, Inc. • Nashville

LEADING FROM THE LOCKERS: STUDENT EDITION

Copyright © 2001 by Injoy Inc.

Illustrations by Bobby Gombert © 2001 Bobby Gombert

Based on John C. Maxwell's *Developing the Leader Within You.*

Special thanks to Ron Luce and Teen Mania for providing research materials for this book.

Published in Nashville, Tennessee, by Tommy Nelson®, a division of Thomas Nelson, Inc.

Unless otherwise indicated, Scripture quotations are from the *International Children's Bible®, New Century Version®,* copyright © 1983, 1986, 1988.

Library of Congress Cataloging-in-Publication Data

Maxwell, John C., 1947–
    Leading from the lockers / John C. Maxwell with Jean Fischer.—Student ed.
        p. cm.
    ISBN 0-8499-7722-3
    1. Leadership—Religious aspects—Christianity—Juvenile literature. [1. Leadership—Religious aspects—Christianity. 2. Christian life.] I. Fischer, Jean, 1952– II. Title.

BV4597.53.L43 F57 2001
248.8'3—dc21

2001030964

Printed in the United States of America
02 03 04 05 PHX 9 8 7 6 5 4 3 2

Contents

Foreword

It's Time to Get Salty

As I travel all over the country every weekend speaking with thousands of young people, I constantly see the effects of a generation that has been led by rock and roll, peer pressure, and by people with no solid foundation in God. As a result, we have a generation of young people who are hurt, who are broken, who are confused, and who are in turn hurting each other.

It is time for a new generation of young people who are believers in Christ to rise up and begin to grow into the leaders of their generation. It is time for every Christian young person to realize that we must be the salt of the earth (Matthew 5:13–16). What Jesus is referring to is that we must be the ones who flavor everything we do with the reality that Jesus is alive! We can't just sit in a church, be a good person, and then go to heaven. While we are on this earth, we must flavor it to be more like Christ. Right now, you can begin to exert leadership in your school or on your ball team. Either you influence those around you, or you get influenced by them. It is time now while you are young to begin to grow into a leader.

But How?

So the big question is, how do we become these kinds of leaders, these kinds of influencers? When I was young I wanted to lead but I had no idea how. How does a person become student body president or the guy on the ball team that everybody looks up to and listens to? Well, the mystery of how to become leaders is taken away in this book you are about to read.

Foreword

In this book, Dr. Maxwell gives you a simple step-by-step plan to get you to be the one who sets the pace for your class, for your Sunday school, or for your locker room. Dr. Maxwell has focused for years on practical ways to help those who love God to be the ones to flavor their environment. I have read almost every one of his books and they have helped shape me as a person and as a leader.

As you read each word, do the exercises in each chapter of this book. It will help you become the leader that God needs you to be, and as you do that, you will influence your world for Christ and make it a better place for everyone. What you are about to read in this book is not just more information, it is specifically designed to make you very, very salty in a world that so desperately needs the influence of somebody who loves God.

—Ron Luce
President / CEO
Teen Mania
Acquire the Fire

Introduction

"**W**hen I grow up, I want to be . . ." (How would you finish this sentence?) In kindergarten, your little hand probably flew up as you and your classmates shouted your confident answers: Firefighter! Doctor! Lawyer! Pilot! Forest ranger! Biophysicist! (Okay, maybe that one was a stretch.) But as we grow older, doubt may begin to creep in. You may start asking yourself: "Can I really be all that I want to be?"

Don't Give Up Your Dreams

Your dreams are important. They are important to you, to those who love you, and to God. Dreams will help you keep going when you are tired, discouraged, or unsure of yourself. And leadership skills are an important key to achieving your dreams. If you learn early in life how to lead, not only are you likely to succeed, but you can also have the joy of helping others succeed.

Think about it. A coach is a leader who has the opportunity to help his players become the best they can be. If a football (baseball, basketball, soccer, or volleyball) team is not winning, sometimes the coach replaces a player or two. But when the *whole team* is having trouble, usually a new coach is hired!

You Can Learn to Be a Leader

Some tourists were visiting a charming village in another country. As they walked by an old man sitting beside a fence, one tourist asked in a rather snobbish way, "Were any great men born in this village?"

The old man replied, "Nope, only babies."

His point is clear. Many of us think we have to be born gifted. Actually, *all* of us are born *babies*. We develop abilities as we grow. Although some of us by nature may find it easier to lead, anyone who really wants to can learn the skills that make a good leader. I have seen this to be true over and over again. You can learn to influence others positively about things that are important to you—your faith, your values, your goals.

The World Needs Good Leaders

Some of us might be tempted just to sit back and let others lead for us. But God wants to use all of us, as Christians, to lead others to Him. He calls us the salt of the earth, the light of the world, a city on a hill. That sounds like leadership to me.

—John C. Maxwell

1
You Can Be a Leader

Hey, You! God's Calling

If I asked you to name some great leaders, who would be on your list? Jesus, the Son of God, was a great leader, and so was Mother Teresa. The president of your country is a leader, and so is Oprah Winfrey, who spiraled from a talk show host to owner of her own corporation. Your pastor, your coach, and your teachers are all leaders. But what about someone like you? Guess what? You can be a leader, too.

> "A LEADER TAKES PEOPLE WHERE THEY WANT TO GO. A GREAT LEADER TAKES PEOPLE WHERE THEY DON'T NECESSARILY WANT TO GO, BUT OUGHT TO BE."
>
> —ROSALYNN CARTER,
> FORMER FIRST LADY OF
> THE UNITED STATES

Would You Give Away Your Pillow?

Trevor Ferrell was a middle school student who spent most of his spare time playing video games and hanging out with his friends. But, because of a learning disability, Trevor didn't like school much, and he only got average grades. Most people didn't see Trevor as anyone special—but God did. He knew Trevor had what it takes to be a good leader.

God's call to Trevor came one night when Trevor was watching TV. On the news, he saw people living on the streets in Philadelphia. How could that be? This is America, and Trevor thought that only happened in places like India. He asked his dad about it, and his dad said it was true. It was December and icy cold in Pennsylvania, where Trevor lived, but nearby, homeless people slept on hard sidewalks, in corners, and over grates, anywhere they could find a tiny bit of heat to keep warm.

*Trevor knew he had to do something. He wanted to go downtown right away to give someone on the streets a blanket and his favorite pillow. So, that's what he did! Trevor and his parents went—**THAT VERY NIGHT**—to the cold winter streets where there were people who had no place else to go. It changed the Ferrell family forever.*

Trevor's enthusiasm, spirit, and drive kept his campaign going. He didn't stop with that first blanket and pillow. When his family ran out of blankets and spare clothing, he put up a sign in his dad's store asking for help. Soon, contributions of food, clothing, and money poured in from all over the city for these forgotten people whom Trevor and his family had come to know by name.

So you see, God called Trevor to be a leader. And He could be calling you, too.

Sorry, Wrong Number

Sometimes, young people don't believe they can be leaders because they don't think adults see them as leaders. Often that includes the people who know them very well.

Imagine if Trevor had told God that night He had the wrong number. What if Trevor had looked the other way and said:

"What can someone my age do anyway?"

That's how some young people react when they think God might be calling them to do something.

And then, there are young people such as Jennifer Howitt. She listened when God called, even though it seemed like a wrong number.

Jennifer's Story

Jennifer was paralyzed after breaking her back in a hiking accident at age nine. Jennifer will probably be in a wheelchair for the rest of her life. She has fought hard to become one of the country's top young disabled athletes. She participated in the track and field competition at the 1998 World Athletic Championships. Then she went to the 2000 Sydney Paralympics as the youngest member of a twelve-person U.S. women's wheelchair basketball team. Jennifer's goal is to show young girls with disabilities that they can achieve whatever they want to. "Maybe you'll have to adapt your goal," she says. "But you can always achieve it." Jennifer listened when God called, and Jennifer became a leader.

You May Even Be a King!

The Lord said to Samuel, ". . . Fill your container with olive oil and go. I am sending you to Jesse who lives in Bethlehem. I have chosen one of his sons to be king."

Samuel saw Eliab. Samuel thought, "Surely the Lord has appointed this person standing here before him." But the Lord said to Samuel, "Don't look at how handsome Eliab is. Don't look at how tall he is. I have not chosen him. God does not see the same way people see. People look at the outside of a person, but the Lord looks at the heart."

Jesse had seven of his sons pass by Samuel. But Samuel said to him, "The Lord has not chosen any of these." Then he asked Jesse, "Are these all the sons you have?"

Jesse answered, "I still have the youngest son. He is out taking care of the sheep."

Samuel said, "Send for him. We will not sit down to eat until he arrives."

So Jesse sent and had his youngest son brought in. He was a fine boy, tanned and handsome.

The Lord said to Samuel, "Go! Appoint him. He is the one."

So Samuel took the container of olive oil. Then he poured oil on Jesse's youngest son to appoint him in front of his brothers. From that day on, the Lord's Spirit entered David with power.

—1 SAMUEL 16:1, 6–7, 10–13

It's easy to think, *God must have the wrong number!*

But the truth is, God often calls young people to lead, and sometimes in the most unlikely circumstances.

Young People Rule!

Those who knew David didn't see him as king material. They didn't believe he was mature enough to rule. Samuel didn't believe it. He thought one of David's older brothers would be king. In fact, David's own father didn't even think David was the right person for the job. His youngest son was, after all, just an inexperienced and unpolished shepherd boy. And you can bet David's brothers didn't see him as a leader. OUR KID BROTHER, DAVID, A KING?! I'm sure they laughed themselves sick.

One day, David arrived on the battlefield and offered to fight the giant Goliath. No one believed he could be serious—not his brothers, not King Saul, and especially not the giant! But David faced the situation head-on. HE KNEW HE HAD BEEN CALLED, and he set out to do the job God wanted him to do.

So, who recognized David as a leader? God did. And that's all that mattered. David proved himself over and over to be the leader God said he was.

Molds Are for Jell-O

What made David stand out as a leader?

DAVID BELIEVED IN HIMSELF, AND HE ANSWERED GOD'S CALL.

Think of a well-known older person whom you admire. Did you think of someone famous like golfer Tiger Woods or singer Celine Dion? Or maybe the person you thought about is a favorite author or a leader in your community. Can you imagine being as important as that person is? Sometimes we forget that the reason these celebrities are important or famous is because they believe in themselves and they get the job done.

What's inside us—what we think of ourselves—can keep us from being great leaders. If we don't go as far as we can go, it could be

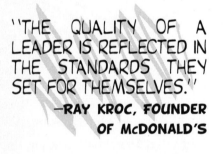

"THE QUALITY OF A LEADER IS REFLECTED IN THE STANDARDS THEY SET FOR THEMSELVES."
—RAY KROC, FOUNDER OF McDONALD'S

because we think we have to fit a certain mold—a picture we carry in our head of what a leader is like. For example, you might think a leader is *always:* wealthy, famous, perfect, from the "right" side of town, from a certain ethnic group . . . the list goes on and on. But if you think that way, you're **wrong.** A leader can be anyone. God's leaders don't have to be pastors or missionaries who work in a church or in a foreign country. They can be young people such as Trevor and Jennifer, and **YOU!** Many leaders make a difference right in their own backyard!

Wanna know what makes a good leader? Try this: When you're

How about Hadassah?

The Bible is full of stories about unlikely leaders. Have you read the Book of Esther yet? It's a cool story about a woman who never dreamed that she would be queen. No one would have guessed God would choose Esther to lead. She was not born to royalty. Her real name was Hadassah, and she was an orphan who lived with her uncle. Add to that the fact she was not the "right" race. She was Hebrew, and the Hebrews were captives of war—aliens—in Persia. In those days, it was as likely that an alien from outer space would be queen as it was that Esther would.

But then something happened—something that had never happened before. There was a search for the most beautiful women in the kingdom. They were ordered to come to the palace, and the king—whose name was Xerxes—would decide which one of them would become the next queen of Persia. And whom did he choose? Esther! And because she became queen, all of the Hebrews were saved from being killed by the Persians.

God didn't care that Esther didn't fit the mold of the woman who would be queen. He saw beyond what was on the surface, and He called Esther to be a great leader.

eating lunch with your friends, ask them what makes a good leader. You'll probably get lots of different answers. There is no such thing as one kind of leader. When it comes to leadership, one size doesn't fit all. God wants to use His leaders in schools, in sports, in art and music activities, in youth groups, in hobbies, in part-time jobs— everywhere!

What's in Your Locker?

Young people are getting involved as leaders in their church groups, schools, and communities. Together, they are finding lots of creative ways to help others and to do good and positive things.

So, what's in your locker? Like any locker, your locker is crammed full of things—some you may never have noticed, some may have dropped down into a black hole, some have been long forgotten, and some you still need to add. As you look in your locker, it may surprise you what you already own and how rapidly you can add to your locker. If you're already a leader, this book will help you shape your skills; if you don't know yet what you've been chosen to lead, these lockers will prepare you for when the day comes—and it will arrive sooner than you think.

ALL AROUND THE WORLD, YOUNG PEOPLE ARE MAKING A DIFFERENCE.

Get some paper, or a notebook, and a pen. We'll call this your locker notebook. As you read through this book, you'll see activities to do in your locker notebook, but you can also use this notebook for your leadership notes.

Your First Leadership Locker

Think of three ways that you would like to lead and write them inside your locker notebook. Think big! What would you like to do right now? How far would you like to go in the future? The locker above has some examples to get you started.

Okay, maybe a cure for cancer is far-fetched at this stage, but you might be the one to discover it later! How could you start now preparing to cure cancer some day? By studying science. Reading about the newest discoveries in medicine. Learning the basics. That's how scientists get started. One small step at a time.

You Could Be a Leader!

There are several reasons why young people are called by God to lead. Which ones apply to you?

You Speak Best for and to Your Peers

Imagine you are unhappy about the quality of food in the school cafeteria at lunchtime. You want the issue brought before the student council. Let's say you can choose any one person from your community to present your case at the next student council meeting. Would you choose one of your classmates who eats the same cafeteria food you do, or would you choose someone who graduated from your middle school twenty years ago?

Your peers on the student council would be more likely to listen to someone in their own generation—someone who shares the same experiences they do.

Every generation has its own leaders, those who share the same history. Moses led the Israelites

"THEN WOLVES WILL LIVE IN PEACE WITH LAMBS. AND LEOPARDS WILL LIE DOWN TO REST WITH GOATS. CALVES, LIONS AND YOUNG BULLS WILL EAT TOGETHER. AND A LITTLE CHILD WILL LEAD THEM."

—ISAIAH 11:6

out of Egypt, but Joshua led them into the Promised Land. Joshua had influence over this new generation because he grew up wandering in the desert just as his peers did. So it was Joshua whom God called to lead the younger generation into the Promised Land.

You are growing up in a time of rapidly changing technology. Cell phones, pagers, computers, digital cameras are all things you are comfortable using to communicate with your peers. But can you imagine your great-grandparents using these things? Innovations change with time, and so does the way we talk.

Every generation has had its own language. (If you don't believe me, ask your mom and dad and your grandma and grandpa.)

The boxed sayings are from other generations, and they may seem

How many of these sayings have you heard?

"Don't have a cow!"   1950s

"That's groovy!"   1970s

"Dig, Daddy-O!"   1960s

"Let it all hang out!"   1980s

strange to you. Now think of sayings in your own generation that might be difficult to communicate to someone older.

God knows which leaders can speak best in certain situations. He made us and He knows what we're like and what we need. You can learn from leaders of any age, but when God chooses young people to lead their own generation, it is often because they communicate best with their peers because they share the same experiences and language.

> "There are admirable potentialities in every human being. Believe in your strength and your youth."
>
> —Andre Gide, author

Being Cool!

When God starts something, He often uses young people. Samuel became a prophet as a small boy. Timothy was very young when he began to lead the church at Ephesus. Even the great apostle John—who wrote the Gospel of John and the Book of Revelation—was a teenager when Jesus invited him to drop everything and become His disciple. In fact, Jesus Himself was very young when He was first recognized as a great leader.

Throughout church history the list of teen leaders goes on: Saint Augustine, John Wesley, John Calvin, Charles Spurgeon, and today, Ron Luce of Teen Mania. You may not even know some of these names, but they are all great leaders.

Jesus Was a Tween, Too

Luke, chapter 2, tells a story about when Jesus and His parents went to Jerusalem for the Passover Feast. Jesus was just twelve years old. The feast lasted for several days, and when it was over, the people went home. They all left together, so there was a great crowd of them traveling at once. Mary and Joseph didn't worry that Jesus wasn't walking with them. They figured He was among their family and friends. But when a whole day passed without seeing Him, they worried. Unable to find Him, they went back to Jerusalem. For three days, they searched. Can you imagine how frantic they were, unable to find their son? Then, finally, they found Him sitting in the temple with the religious leaders, listening, and asking questions. The grown-up leaders were amazed that this young person was so understanding and wise. Little did they know that Jesus, the Son of God, was sent to be the greatest leader of all.

Your Whole Life Is Ahead of You

My...the golden years sure are changing.

With medical technology moving at breakneck speed, YOU COULD LIVE TO BE 100 OR BEYOND! Just think of all the people you'll meet in your lifetime.

Some experts estimate that the average person influences at least ten thousand people during his lifetime. If a person begins to lead at a very young age, the number of people he can influence will be much higher. Imagine having sixty to ninety years to serve God! Just think of how many people will influence you during your life. Better yet, think of all the

> "I AM ALWAYS DOING THAT WHICH I CAN NOT DO, IN ORDER THAT I MAY LEARN HOW TO DO IT."
>
> —PABLO PICASSO, ARTIST

people whom *you* will influence. **GOD WANTS TO REACH THE WHOLE WORLD**—and He wants to use young people to do it.

When you begin leading as a young person, you have time to grow and learn from everything you do, including your successes and mistakes. And you will have years of experience in leading before most people even begin to think about it! That's awesome.

Doing the Impossible!

Young people are much more likely to believe in and go after the "impossible" than most older folks who have been hardened by the world. It's easy to give up hope sometimes, when you've seen so many bad things happen to good people. But God wants leaders who see nothing but hope—He wants leaders who simply **believe things can be done**.

Dr. Martin Luther King Jr.

As a young man Martin Luther King Jr. believed in peace and equality for all races. Dr. King persevered against those who said it would never work, and eventually he caused people in the United States to take action against moral injustice. He had a dream for a better future and believed he could make a difference— and he did! He answered God's call, and he became a great leader; God made him a great man by building on his never-ending faith. The call he answered changed the world for the better for **YOU,** *because* **YOU ARE THE FUTURE.**

What will you do for those who come after you?

Jesus said, "The greatest person in the kingdom of heaven is the one who makes himself humble like this child" (Matthew 18:4). He was saying that young people are open to fresh, new ideas. Young people see the opportunities that are ahead instead of the obstacles.

You Are Enthusiastic and Determined

Have you ever nagged and nagged your parents until they agreed to let you go to the mall, or stay out a little later, or maybe spend the night at a friend's house? (Now, tell the truth.) You kept at it until you got what you wanted, didn't you? That may not be the greatest thing to do when it comes to your parents, but that kind of determination *used for God* can be very valuable. ENTHUSIASM, IDEALISM, FOCUS, ENERGY—these are all things young people can use to answer God's call.

Remember Jennifer Howitt? She had to learn to live without being able to walk. That was hard! It took *lots* of determination and energy. But Jennifer kept at it until she was as comfortable in her wheelchair as she had been on her own two feet. Jennifer was determined not to let her disability get in her way. And that's just the kind of attitude that God loves in a leader.

You Are Unpolished and Inexperienced

That sounds like a put-down, doesn't it? But really it's not. Let's look at it from God's point of view. The Bible says God is the potter and you are the clay. God wants to take you just as you are and make you into something wonderful. If you start out knowing nothing, and God gives you the ability to do something great, then God gets all the glory. And that's what God wants. He wants to polish you and make you into something special. He wants to use you to help Him accomplish good works.

Think again about Trevor Ferrell. Trevor started out not knowing anything about the homeless in his hometown. But by the time he had finished the sixth grade, Trevor's story had been told in the *New York Times, Boston Globe, Chicago Tribune, Philadelphia Inquirer, USA Today, People* magazine, *McCall's* magazine, and on all the major television networks. He was honored at the White House by then-President Ronald Reagan. Just think about what Trevor was able to accomplish when he decided to *do* something and answer God's call.

BEING YOUNG IS WHAT MADE ALL THE DIFFERENCE. If Trevor had been an adult, few would have noticed his work with the homeless, even if he did a very good job. But what made his accomplishments different was that Trevor was a young person just like you and your friends. He was not famous or the son of someone famous. In fact, very few people knew Trevor outside of his circle of family and friends and teachers. What made Trevor special was that a young person couldn't do what Trevor did without God's help. God took someone unpolished and inexperienced, and He made him a leader. In a way, Trevor is a modern-day King David. He went from being an ordinary boy to becoming someone who really made a difference. It began with a simple act: Trevor offered someone his own pillow. Even though his ministry grew and met the needs of many homeless people, Trevor was still a young person. He never stopped doing things in the simple way a young person would do them. And that's just the point! Only God—working through Trevor—could accomplish this work. Trevor just answered God's call and allowed God to do the rest. That was enough. God knows young people are cool, and He knows He can count on them to get the job done.

Don't Hang Up

Do you think of yourself as a leader? You can lead, you know, and you will lead—if you listen, prepare yourself to lead, and answer when God calls you. Look around your home, your church, your school, and your community. Where are you needed and how can you help? Your moment will arrive. Some day, God will call you to lead, so keep your eyes and ears open—and don't hang up!

Sign Me Up!

Copy the following prayer in your locker notebook. When you feel that God is calling you to lead, sign it and date it. Is God calling you right now? You never know. **HAVE YOU BEEN LISTENING?** God might be calling you to take a first step and do something simple like Trevor did when he gave away his favorite pillow. Small acts of leadership often grow. When God calls you to lead, make a list in your locker notebook of how you are answering His call.

Maybe you're not ready to sign this today. That's okay, too. Keep it in your notebook and sign it later. How you will lead and when are between you and God, but be sure to think and pray about it often.

Leader's Prayer

I want to follow You, God, wherever You want me to go. I hear You calling my name, asking me to serve You as a leader. I am willing to answer Your call. Work through me, Lord, to make good things happen.

*Name*_____

*Date*_____

2
Stop and Take Notice

Things Are Looking Up

You've probably seen New York City, "the Big Apple," on TV or in movies. It's a place where few people stand still. And if somebody does, he or she is sure to be noticed eventually.

One day, a man in New York City stood on a busy street corner. He just stood there looking up at the sky. It was rush hour in the city, so it was a long time before anyone noticed him standing there, but once he was noticed, he got lots of attention. Soon a crowd gathered around the man, and all the people began to stretch their necks to try to see what he saw. Was the Stealth bomber flying overhead? Was a bad storm on the way? Did he see Jesus in the clouds coming back for His people? No matter how hard the people looked, they couldn't see anything unusual. They jammed in closer to the man to make sure they were looking in the right direction. They shielded their eyes from the sun, and they squinted harder into the distance. One person even took out a pair of binoculars! But no one else could see what it was that captured the man's attention.

New Yorkers don't often talk to strangers, but, finally, one man could no longer stand the suspense. ''HEY, MAN,'' he said, ''WHAT ARE YOU LOOKING AT?''

The man was startled. He hadn't even noticed that a crowd had gathered around him. "I'm looking at nothing in particular," he answered—still looking up. "I just have a cramp in my neck."

Okay, so maybe it didn't really happen. But that's an illustration of influence! And influence is an important part of being a leader. One man with a sore neck caused a whole crowd to stop and do what he was doing. He hadn't planned it, but during the time all those people were looking up in the sky, he was their unchallenged leader!

Will the Real Leader Please Stand Up!

When you read chapter 1, you named people whom you admire—those whom you look up to as leaders. Now, I'm going to ask you why those people influenced you. What was it about them that made you stop and take notice? Is it what they looked like, what they wore, what they sounded like that caught your attention? Or did they stand out as leaders because of something they did or a certain way they acted?

He Made a Mouse Famous

In the early part of the twentieth century, God called Walt Disney to be a leader in the family entertainment industry, and **JUST LOOK AT WHAT HE DID!** Disneyland and Disney World . . . Mickey Mouse and Donald Duck . . . children's books, CDs, videos. If you asked all the kids in your school how many of them have seen at least one Disney movie in their

A DOLPHIN CAN EVEN BE A LEADER. WITHIN ONLY A FEW WEEKS IN CAPTIVITY, DOLPHINS CAN INFLUENCE PEOPLE TO STAND ON THE EDGE OF THE POOL AND FEED THEM FISH!

life, would *every* hand go up? That's what I figured. Do you see how Walt Disney influenced the way you and your friends think about the world? His ideas have continued to influence others long after his death.

Not all leaders are good role models. Some leaders even use their influence to lead others in the wrong direction. But the rule is still true:

If People Have Followers, They Are Leaders.

Unlikely Leaders

Think about some other well-known sports players who have been in the news over the past few years because of problems they've created either on or off the court. Some of them may angrily kick a news reporter on camera or head-butt other players on the court. They may

A Leader with Big Shoes to Fill

And what about Michael Jordan? He has probably sold more Nike shoes than any Nike salesman alive. Is that because Michael Jordan knows a lot about manufacturing shoes? No. Do Nikes make Michael Jordan a great basketball player? Not really. HE WOULD BE GREAT IN ANY SHOES, *so long as they were big enough for his feet. But young people (and grownups) buy millions of "Air Jordan" Nikes because they want to be a sports leader like Michael Jordan is. He has influence.*

not be team players. They may pout when the ref takes them out of the game. They may use illegal drugs or commit other crimes. Are these sports stars leaders? Yes, they are. They are idols to many kids who also want to be great players. Unfortunately, they misuse their influence, suggesting that you can do whatever you want—if you are a famous sports personality. And that kind of influence can lead young people the wrong way.

Are You a Backseat Driver?

What about a person lacking influence? Many people believe, for example, that if you're the captain of your baseball team, you are a leader. But the title "captain" will not make you a leader if the team ignores your ideas. On the other hand, real leaders are followed whether or not they wear a badge that says "captain."

Check it out. Whom does everybody look at when you try to decide what to do when your friends get together? Whom do others agree with when you argue over the rules of a game? Whose clothes does everyone want to copy? It's the REAL LEADER whom people turn to—the one with INFLUENCE. A leader looks the same in your Scout troop, your youth group, your classroom, or your baseball team. The number of followers someone has will tell you whether or not that person is a leader.

Influenza or Influence? Either Way, It's Catching

The Power of influence.

If your best friend has the flu, you might catch it. If someone has influence, that might rub off on you, too. **Influence isn't unusual.** It happens every day. When something or someone is important to you, you always remember him, no matter how much time passes. And sometimes you even integrate the things you admire about him into your own personality. That's fine as long as his influence is positive and good.

Sometimes, major events influence a whole generation. Wars can kill people's brothers, sisters, sons, and daughters, changing those families forever. School shootings alter the way schools operate. A presidential election affects the course of a nation. But more often, it's the little things that people say or do that influence you the most—including those TV commercials that make you think you'll be totally square if you don't own a certain game or wear a certain style of makeup or clothes.

No matter what you do, you will influence others. They will remember the things you do and say. Sometimes that's a good thing, and sometimes, well . . . it's not so great. *It all depends on you.*

Today the Neighborhood, Tomorrow the World

It's true that people influence the people around them, so what kind of influence are you now? What kind of influence would you like to be? That's an important thing to think about. Who are your role models? How have they influenced you? How will you influence others by what you've learned from them?

To the Finish Line

Jeff Gordon, NASCAR champion, knows that many young people look up to him because he is FAST on the racetrack, so he works hard to be a good Christian role model for them to follow off the racetrack as well as on. When Jeff wins a race, he cracks open a Pepsi in the winner's circle rather than celebrating with beer or champagne. He also spends many hours working with charities and speaking to Christian gatherings about his love for Jesus Christ. Why? Because Jeff knows he has influence, and he wants to use his influence in a positive way.

Players and Prayers

When I was in high school, I played basketball. After I made a commitment to Christ, I used to walk into the locker room after games and just sit there alone, to have a little prayer time. I thought no one was watching.

One day, my coach came in and saw me. "Are you all right?" he asked.

"I'm okay, Coach. I'm just having a little prayer time, thanking God for the game tonight," I responded quietly. I didn't try to make a show of it or come across as some holy man.

Evidently, my coach never forgot that little conversation. Fourteen years later, after I had become a pastor and was well into my career, he had a crisis in his life. He contacted me, and we talked. That's when he said to me, "John—I have watched you play, and I have watched you pray. I need what you have."

That day I got to lead my high school basketball coach to the Lord. You never know where your influence might spread.

Your Race

Maybe you feel you don't have as much influence with others as you would like. You can change that. You have to be patient and learn to share your ideas and learn to express your ideas clearly. **DON'T PUSH,** and others will listen to what you have to say. One of the best ways to learn how to influence is to teach someone how to do something. Make sure to give clear instructions, though, or your student won't do it right! And you want to make sure that you're not a BOSSY leader.

It may sound funny that you gain in influence the more *humble* you are, but it's true. Giving of yourself and making sacrifices stretches your ability to influence others.

Good Samaritan

Eighteen-year-old Kristen Watson was driving home from a fun day at an amusement park. Before long, she came upon the scene of an accident in which a little girl, who had been delivering newspapers, was hit by a truck. Kristen stopped her car and hurried over to help the little girl. She tried to keep her calm until she could be airlifted to a hospital where she would receive treatment for head and neck injuries.

Imagine the influence Kristen had on that frightened little kid! Kristen's influence continued to grow as she gave of herself to other people. She went on to become an

LEADERSHIP IS INFLUENCE. AND INFLUENCE IS LEADERSHIP.

apprentice firefighter and certified emergency medical technician. But the way she influenced others didn't stop there. Her volunteer efforts with young kids—from the Special Olympics to the Boy Scouts—earned her Connecticut's Youth Spirit Award for 2000. Kristen's story is an illustration that if everyone spent a little time giving back, the world would be a much better place.

Your Influence

So what can you do? Look around you and see who needs help. How about the kid who always sits alone on the school bus? What about the elderly woman who lives across the street and is all by herself? And don't just look for people outside your family. You can give of yourself in simple ways, such as playing a "dumb" baby game with your little brother or sister—especially when you have something more **FUN** to do.

What you say and what you do influences others in either a positive or a negative way. The more you reach out to others in a good way, the more others want to follow you and **BE JUST LIKE YOU**. And you will also find many wonderful friends you might have missed by always doing the same things and hanging out with the same crowd. Reaching out has lots of advantages.

Who's in Charge? Guess What, It's You!

It's time to take a look inside some lockers and find out about levels of leadership. Then we'll stuff the lockers with things you'll want to remember!

Leadership Locker 1

The first locker is for whoever is in charge. The **position** locker holds up the rest. It's the bottom locker, and it provides the foundation for the other leadership lockers. LEADERSHIP BEGINS WITH A LEADER—someone who influences others. And it's the leader's job to hold up the rest of the team.

Suppose, for example, that your neighbors hire you and your little sister to mow, weed, and rake their yard every week for one summer. The deal is that you will be paid more to supervise the work and make sure everything is done correctly. That means you are in charge—you are the leader—of the yard crew. Your sister has to do what you say because the neighbors told her you were in charge.

Will your friend down the street weed your neighbor's yard, if you tell him to? No way! He's not a part of the team you lead. And your sister will probably only do what you tell her to do if it has to do with the neighbor's yard. Just see what will happen if you tell her what to do when the

A Bossy Leader

- ☐ Tells people what to do
- ☐ Depends on his or her power
- ☐ Makes others afraid
- ☐ Thinks about himself
- ☐ Blames others when things don't work right

A CARING LEADER

- ☐ Teaches people what they need to know
- ☐ Depends on good relationships
- ☐ Makes others excited about what they do
- ☐ Thinks about the group
- ☐ Finds ways to fix the problem

31

two of you are washing dishes tonight. She'll be very quick to remind you that she only has to do what you say when she is working on your yard crew! So you—a quick learner—can see that being in charge means you are the leader only of specific people in a specific situation.

It's great that you're in charge, isn't it? But how do the people you're in charge of feel about it? Do they see you as a **great leader**? Be honest now. Are you leading people, or are you bossing them around? A bossy person and a good leader are very different. And followers will react to them in different ways. Look at the descriptions on page 31 and you'll see what I mean.

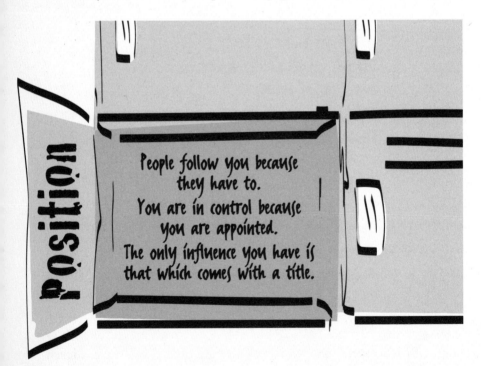

Position

People follow you because they have to.
You are in control because you are appointed.
The only influence you have is that which comes with a title.

What kind of a leader do you want to be? How are you going to get there? As you grow in influence, you will be able to lead more people in more situations. But it's wise to start at the beginning. Be careful not to run ahead too fast and skip the first step of "being in charge." You will learn more than you ever thought you could if you follow the leadership levels in order. Don't skip any of the lockers. Remember that the position locker holds up all the others. If you put nothing in it, the lockers on top of it will come crashing down—just like a leader who skips some leadership steps along the way.

Now, stuff the position locker with what you have learned.

At the first level of leadership— position —you are in charge because you have been appointed to a leadership position. You might be in charge of a fund-raising event for your school or church, or you might be appointed to a student council office. At this level, others follow you because they have to. You haven't done anything yet to influence them to keep on following you.

Leadership Locker 2: It's Cool to Be Cool

This next locker—the permission locker—balances on top of the position locker. To get it to balance correctly, you have to fill it with all the right things.

Sometimes a person never outgrows being a bossy leader. Sometimes, a bossy leader becomes a BULLY. But a bully can make others follow him only if he is stronger than they are. This kind of leader is like a chicken in a ''PECKING ORDER.''

THE TALE OF THE EVIL CHICKEN

In any group of chickens, there is a number **1** *hen. Imagine the meanest, nastiest hen on God's earth—we'll call her* **EViL CHiCKEN.** *This chicken usually bullies all the other hens in the henhouse—and they run when they see her coming. It's too bad that chickens can't fly, or these chickens would be long gone. There are rules to Evil Chicken's little game. She can peck any other hen, but none of the other hens can peck her. Evil Chicken is one of those bossy, bully leaders we've already talked about.*

The other chickens in the group fall in behind Evil Chicken in decreasing order of nastiness. The number **2** *chicken can peck all of the chickens except Evil Chicken. The number* **3** *chicken can peck every other chicken except Evil Chicken and the number* **2** *chicken. And so it goes down the line, ending with one poor little hen everyone pecks on—but she doesn't get to peck on anyone.*

You can check out the pecking order principle by visiting a chicken farm. It does work. But take it from me, if you use this method to lead other people, sooner or later you're going to run into an Evil Chicken bigger than you who will make sure you end up wearing a helmet!

*So, what happens when you encounter an Evil Chicken? Do you stand up to her, or do you run away? Chickens aren't smart enough to know they have leadership choices—***BUT YOU ARE!*** You might decide to confront the Evil Chicken. (Which could be a bad idea, unless you did it the right way—check out chapter 10 for ideas on how to confront people or chickens, for that matter.) In the meantime, you can concentrate on* **NOT BEiNG A BOSSY LEADER.** *You want followers walking behind you, not running after you with beaks wide open.*

A leader at the **permission** level doesn't lead by being bossy. She leads by liking and helping others. She is not interested at all in a pecking order. People follow her because they want to, not because they have to.

Your followers will do what you say when you're in charge because they have to. But before anyone follows you *willingly,* he must know you care about him as a person. That's what makes you cool. But you can't fake it. People can tell right away if you're insincere. You see, *true leadership begins with the heart,* not the head. They won't follow you very long just because you're good at something or wear neat clothes.

Bill Cosby, Mr. Influence

Have you ever watched Bill Cosby talk to little kids? They will tell him things they wouldn't even tell their best friends—and they even do it before a TV camera! Why? Because Bill gets down to their level, and he looks them in the eye. He understands and speaks their language. He knows their thoughts and feelings. He smiles and laughs *with* them, not at them. Bill Cosby makes kids feel important, and that's why **KiDS WOULD FOLLOW HiM TO THE MOON.** Bill is cool, and he is a good role model to imitate, if you want people to know you care. Someone like Bill Cosby has a very positive influence on others.

> "YOU CAN TURN PAINFUL SITUATIONS AROUND THROUGH LAUGHTER. IF YOU CAN FIND HUMOR IN ANYTHING—EVEN POVERTY—YOU CAN SURVIVE IT."
>
> —BiLL COSBY, ENTERTAINER

So, let's stuff the **PERMISSION** locker above with what you've just learned. This locker **BALANCES** on top of the position locker. Stuff it carefully with what you've learned, or it will come tumbling down.

At the second leadership level—**permission**—your followers are there because they want to follow you. You've proven you aren't a bossy leader and that you care about people. They trust you, and they will follow wherever you lead them. You have INFLUENCE!

Leadership Locker 3:
You're the One Who Makes Things Happen

The **PRODUCTION** locker is the top locker. It's like the top person in a cheerleaders' pyramid. It's a tough job to balance way up there, but you're a good leader, and you can do it. This is the locker that has all the good stuff inside.

So far, you're cool, and people like to be around you. You have influence in a lot of situations. HEY, YOU'RE A LEADER! Why not just stay where you are and enjoy it? The answer is this: After a while, hanging out with friends gets boring. One by one, your followers will leave you to follow someone who is getting things done. So what happens now? Do you just sit there and let everyone leave? No. Now you move up to the next level of leadership—YOU MAKE THINGS HAPPEN.

If you've been a caring leader, your followers already like and trust you and are willing to do what you tell them to do. Remember, I said earlier that you should carefully think about what kind of influence you want to have. It is especially important at the production level, because now you get to **put your influence to use**. You can do good things with it and make the world a better place, or you can lead people in the wrong way and add to the troubles of our society. I think I already know which way you'll choose.

Suppose your science club elects you the vice president. Every year the club has a car wash to make money for trips. As vice president, you are in charge of running the whole thing. Maybe in the past, the members didn't want to work on the car wash because the leader was bossy and hurt their feelings. But this year, everyone in the club shows up because they know you can make work fun. Everyone seems to get along when you lead. **Aren't you cool!** When the group runs out of soap, they come to you because you'll know what to do. If it looks like it might rain, they know you'll find a way to persuade people to get their cars washed anyway. Because you know how to get things done, this year the car wash makes more money than it ever has before. (I told you this was fun! Don't you feel good about yourself right now?)

All of the hard work you put into learning how to influence others

THIS IS WHEN LEADERSHIP BEGINS TO BE FUN!

People follow you because they like you and what you are doing.

You are good at fixing problems.

You've built a successful team.

pays off when you have the satisfaction of a job well done. Everyone wins, and everyone feels good.

So, what should we put into the **production** locker above? Stuff it carefully, because it balances precariously on top of the permission and position lockers. If you're careless here, they all might fall down. And you don't want to have to start over, do you?

IN THIS CHAPTER YOU'VE BEEN GIVEN THE KEYS TO BECOMING A GREAT CHRISTIAN LEADER. THEY WILL HELP OTHERS TRUST AND BELIEVE YOU WHEN YOU TELL THEM ABOUT JESUS CHRIST, THE GREATEST LEADER OF ALL AND THE SON OF GOD. YOU WILL NEVER DO ANYTHING IN LIFE MORE IMPORTANT THAN THAT.

At the **production** level, you are getting things done. You are more than a leader with a position and a title. You're not alone. You have followers. And if you've stuffed the lockers with all the right things and kept them in balance, people are following you because you have influence. **Look what you've done!** You've built a team. Your followers like you and what you're doing, and together the whole bunch of you are working toward some really great goals. **WAY TO GO!**

It Won't Work without Practice

Will you be a great concert bassoonist if you don't practice the bassoon? No, you won't. If you're always late for football practice, will you ever

replace that starting quarterback on your favorite pro team? Probably not. If you don't practice being a good influence, will you ever be a great leader? Never!

Remember, WE ALL HAVE INFLUENCE, and it's up to us to influence others in a positive way.

Think about ways you can practice being a good influence. Suppose everyone in your crowd decides not to wear a helmet when in-line skating, but you see that the little kids on your block are beginning to follow your example. They (and you) could get badly hurt. What could you do to change this situation? Name three people at your school whom you respect as leaders. From what you have learned in this chapter, why do you think they have so many followers? What can you learn from their example?

Set a time this week to teach someone else how to do something you already know how to do, like change a bicycle tire, throw a fastball, or play a new computer game. Not only will you learn to express your ideas clearly, but also you'll make the other person feel important.

A Locker Filled with Care

Now, take out your locker notebook and write at least three things you can do to show you are a caring leader. The locker on page 42 holds some examples.

HEY, LOOK AT YOU NOW! You're becoming a better leader every day. You've gone from knowing little or nothing about leadership to being someone in charge who makes things happen. You have *influence*, AND THAT MAKES YOU COOL!

3
Integrity:
Wearing Yourself Inside Out

When "Finders keepers, losers weepers" becomes a personal motto.

What's Your Final Answer?

Imagine you're walking home from school with some of your classmates, and you're talking about a concert all of you really want to attend. But the tickets are very expensive, and none of you have enough money. Sound familiar? So, the group starts brainstorming ideas on how to earn some cash—really fast. It would take several baby-sitting jobs each just to pay for one ticket, and you need the money too fast for that idea.

Then you spot it. Right there on the sidewalk. A thick white envelope. You pick it up, you look inside, and you find **$300!** There's no name on the envelope and no kind of identification.

"It's a miracle!" one of your classmates yells. "That's enough money to buy all of us tickets and have enough left over to get some CDs."

All of the kids are looking at you, waiting to hear what you have to say. *It's not my envelope,* you think. But now the problem is in your hands, and you have to solve it. Think about the kind of leader you are. You make things happen. That's what makes you such a great leader, and that's why all of these kids are looking at you right now. You also know how to influence people. So, what will you do? What's your final answer?

County fair trivia games.

Moving up the Leadership Ladder

If you decided to try to find the owner of the envelope and give the money back, you've graduated to the next level of leadership—*integrity*.

Integrity is the most important ingredient of leadership. Integrity means standing up for the values and morals you believe in, no matter what. You can explain to your friends that it isn't right to take something that doesn't belong to you. You can tell them the three hundred dollars might be somebody's life savings. To do that would be to act with integrity.

It's Getting Hot in Here

The Bible talks about integrity in Daniel 3:1–30. Three young men, Shadrach, Meshach, and Abednego, who weren't much older than you are now, lived during the reign of King Nebuchadnezzar. In the story, the king, who didn't believe in God, built a big, golden statue in honor of himself. He had such an ego that he wanted everyone in the kingdom to bow down and worship his statue. But Shadrach, Meshach, and Abednego refused.

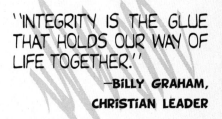

"INTEGRITY IS THE GLUE THAT HOLDS OUR WAY OF LIFE TOGETHER."

—BILLY GRAHAM, CHRISTIAN LEADER

They told Nebuchadnezzar that it was wrong to worship anything but the real God in heaven. When he heard that, the king threatened to throw the young men into a fiery furnace if they didn't obey. But they didn't give in. They stuck to what they believed.

Then, the worst thing happened. Nebuchadnezzar did just what he said he would. He threw the young men into a hot, fiery furnace. But because they stayed true to God and their strong moral values, God saved them from the flames, and they weren't even touched by the fire!

Putting the "Amen" in "Amends"

After I made my commitment to Christ, my life changed dramatically. In fact, I realized I had to make some things right. First, I had to go to Mr. Galliher of Galliher's Drug Store and confess that I had stolen a sports magazine. I was totally embarrassed. I paid for the magazine and waited for his response. Fortunately, he was gracious and forgave me.

My next stop was the grocery store not far away. It may seem small today, but I knew I had taken a Dr Pepper from the store. I offered to pay for it and apologized. The grocer, too, was very gracious to me. The more I did this, the easier I found it became.

My final stop was to visit one of my coaches in high school. I returned some practice jerseys, a ball, and a towel. I had taken them during my last two years of playing on the team. I just didn't feel right knowing I had these things. Somehow I knew that if I wanted to be effective and keep a clear conscience in my life, I had to make things right and keep them right! (By the way, all of these gentlemen expressed how pleased they were with me.)

Wearing Yourself Inside Out

Brandon Keefe is a typical barefoot California teen in baggy shorts and T-shirt, but Brandon is anything but ordinary. A few years ago,

Brandon found out that a California children's home wanted books for its library, but there wasn't enough money in the budget to buy them. Brandon had an idea for how to get the job done—a book drive.

The next day he presented the idea to his class at school. But Brandon's idea didn't stop there. He distributed fliers, talked to classmates, and got his whole school involved in a book drive that collected more than eight hundred children's

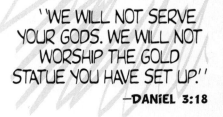

''WE WILL NOT SERVE YOUR GODS. WE WILL NOT WORSHIP THE GOLD STATUE YOU HAVE SET UP.''
—DANIEL 3:18

books for the California home. In the years since, Brandon hasn't given up. So far, he's collected almost ten thousand books to give to charity.

Is Brandon a leader? Sure he is! He didn't just talk about doing something. He did it! And that's integrity. A person with integrity is the same on the inside as on the outside. He is who he says he is, and he does what he says he'll do.

Taking on the World

Samantha Smith was another young person who had integrity. She let the whole world know what she was like on the inside.

Samantha was worried about world peace, but instead of just talking about it with her family and friends, she did something about it. In 1983, when Samantha was ten years old, she wrote a letter to then-Soviet leader Yuri Andropov asking what he planned to do to keep peace. This is what she wrote:

Dear Mr. Andropov,

My name is Samantha Smith. I am ten years old. Congratulations on your new job. I have been worrying about Russia and the United States getting into a nuclear war. Are you going to vote to have a war or not? If you aren't, please tell me how you are going to help to not have a war. This question you do not have to answer, but I would like to know why you want to conquer the world or at least our country. God made the world for us to live together in peace and not to fight.

Sincerely,
Samantha Smith

Samantha received a response. A portion of it said:

Dear Samantha,

. . . You write that you are anxious about whether there will be a nuclear war between our two countries. And you ask are we doing anything so that war will not break out. . . . I will reply to you seriously and honestly.

Yes, Samantha, we in the Soviet Union are trying to do everything so that there will not be war on earth. . . . Soviet people well know what a terrible thing war is. Forty-two years ago, Nazi Germany, which strived for supremacy over the whole world, attacked our country, burned and destroyed many thousands of our towns and villages, killed millions of Soviet men, women, and children. In that war, which ended with our victory, we were in alliance with the United States: Together we fought for the liberation of many. . . . And today we want very much to live in peace. . . . And certainly with such a great country as the United States of America.

Integrity: Wearing Yourself Inside Out

In America and in our country there are nuclear weapons—terrible weapons that can kill millions of people in an instant. But we do not want them to be ever used. That's precisely why the Soviet Union solemnly declared throughout the entire world that never—never—will it use nuclear weapons first against any country. . . .

. . . (In) answer to your second question: "Why do you want to wage war against the whole world or at least the United States?" We want nothing of the kind. No one in our country . . . want either a big or "little" war. We want peace. . . . We want peace for ourselves and for all peoples of the planet, . . . For our children, and for you, Samantha. . . .

Thank you for your letter. I wish you all the best in your young life.

Y. Andropov

Mr. Andropov also invited Samantha to visit him in Moscow. She accepted, and spent two weeks touring the Soviet Union. Samantha's story got lots of attention, and soon almost everyone in America knew about Samantha's letter.

Samantha took action about something she felt was important. She was brave enough to think she could influence one of the most important leaders in the world. And she did!

SADLY, SAMANTHA SMITH WAS KILLED IN A PLANE ACCIDENT IN 1985. BUT NOT BEFORE GOD CALLED HER TO LEAD HER GENERATION IN FINDING WORLD PEACE.

You don't have to go clear across the world to get things done. Every day, young people are finding ways to make a difference in their homes, neighborhoods, and communities. What can you do to help?

What They See Is What You Get

Integrity determines what we do and how others will respond. People will know if you're not wearing your insides on the outside—because your actions will speak louder than your words. Think about it. Are the people you lead more likely to do what you do, or will they do what you say?

Let's say you have a great idea to clean up all the trash that blew into your neighborhood park after a big storm. You organize a group of your friends, tell them what has to be done, and arrange to meet them in the park early Saturday morning. Everyone shows up but you. You decided instead to go to watch your little brother play Little League baseball. Your actions spoke louder than your words. You really didn't care all that much about cleaning up the park. How do you think your friends will react? Will they follow your lead the next time you suggest something?

Not exactly the kind of enthusiasm that inspires greatness.

What if you're the leader of your cheerleading squad, and you lack enthusiasm because the team is so bad? What will happen when you get out on the field to cheer? Answer: Your whole squad will lack enthusiasm because of the attitude of their leader—you. What *they* see is what *you* get. To get the response you want, you have to set the example.

Touched By An Angel

In 1993, a film producer and writer named Martha Williamson was asked to create a television show about angels. Martha, who describes herself proudly as a "committed Christian," soon became the creator and executive producer of the hit CBS series *Touched By An Angel.* Martha wasn't afraid to stand up for her values and beliefs. She created a show about the love of God—a show that wasn't afraid to mention God's name or to tell the world, "God loves you." As a result, *Touched By An Angel* receives thousands of letters each week from people whose lives have been changed by Martha's show.

> "GOD EXISTS. GOD LOVES YOU. GOD WANTS TO BE PART OF OUR LIVES."
>
> —MARTHA WILLIAMSON, TV PRODUCER, IN INTERVIEW WITH *TV GUIDE*

Touched By An Angel might have been a very different television show if Martha had hidden her Christian faith from the show's writers, actors, and viewers.

People with integrity have nothing to hide and nothing to fear. They aren't afraid for others to know what they believe, and they use their morals and values to set a good example—an example that will bring results.

Which Way Are You Going?

Decisions. Decisions.

Have you noticed how hard it can sometimes be to decide between what you want to do and what you ought to do? No one, no matter how "spiritual," no matter if he or she is a young person or old, can avoid making decisions between right and wrong. Integrity determines who we are and how we will respond before a conflict even happens.

Imagine how different things would be at Columbine High School had the events of April 20, 1999, not happened. What if the young gunmen had thought about right and wrong before they fired the shots, or even before they brought guns to school?

Rachel Scott was a student at Columbine that day. She was outside the cafeteria when the gunmen approached her. Rachel was a committed Christian, and news reports later indicated that the young men had singled out some of the Christian students to be killed. They'd made fun of Christian students, and they didn't like them. Before he shot Rachel, one of the shooters asked her if she really believed in God. Rachel answered, "Yes." A split second later, she was in heaven with the Lord.

Rachel faced the toughest conflict of her life. Which way should she go? Should she deny her Christian faith, hoping that she wouldn't be shot? Or should she stand up for her Christian beliefs and face the possibility of death? Rachel did what she believed to be right. She was the same on the inside as she professed to be on the outside—a Christian.

Rachel was a leader, not only because she had integrity, but also because she influenced other young people. Who knows how many young people became Christians or grew in their faith when they heard about what Rachel did? When Pastor Bruce Porter spoke at Rachel Scott's funeral, he noted that "the torch of God's love in Christ" had fallen from Rachel's hand. "Who will take up this torch?" he asked. Hundreds of young people sprang to their feet and held up their arms in agreement.

What about you? What would you have done had you been Rachel Scott?

If you have integrity, you will be consistent, and your beliefs will be mirrored by the way you act. There won't be any difference between what you appear to be and who you really are—no matter how tough the situation.

A Leadership Locker Filled with Trust

Let's look into another leadership locker. This next one is called **TRUST** and is on page 54. Inside your locker notebook, write three things that you think make you trustworthy.

I put the needs of others first.

I am the same on the inside and the outside.

I am honest.

It's time to take a test. I can already hear you: "Oh, no! Not a test!" Calm down; this is easy. It's only three questions—and it's only a "Yes or No" test.

Are you ready? Here's THE TRUST TEST. Say the answers to yourself.

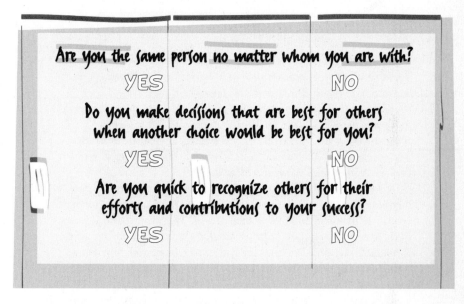

Are you the same person no matter whom you are with?

YES　　　　　　　　　　NO

Do you make decisions that are best for others when another choice would be best for you?

YES　　　　　　　　　　NO

Are you quick to recognize others for their efforts and contributions to your success?

YES　　　　　　　　　　NO

If you answered "yes" to all three questions, then you are a trustworthy leader. If you answered "no," turn around and look behind you. Chances are you won't see anyone following you. For a leader to have the authority to lead, he or she has to have the trust of those who are following.

All of us have known those who were not the same on the outside as they were on the inside. Think about the people at your school. I'm sure you have classmates like that. Or maybe there are sports stars, musicians, or other celebrities whom you thought were one way and who turned out to be another. These people may seem trustworthy on the surface, but on the inside they have only their own interests in mind—and eventually their true colors will show.

Survivor

You probably know about the television show Survivor. *On the show, sixteen castaways—real people—spend weeks living together in a remote wilderness location such as a deserted island or the Australian outback. The "survivors" form their own "tribe." They cooperate to build their own shelter, gather and catch their own food, and participate in* **contests for rewards.** Contests! *This is where integrity comes in. Each week, the tribe meets to vote one of its members off the show. The game is won when only one survivor is left— and the winner takes home a million dollars!*

If you've watched the show, you've seen that the players will do anything to earn their teammates' trust—but the players are not necessarily trustworthy in the way they earn it! That way, they are least likely to be voted off. On the other hand, there is no real loyalty when it comes to the vote. The votes are cast in secret—so you don't know whom you can trust. There are no rules. You can vote anyone off for any reason. Since you—the reader—know a lot about integrity already, you can see that there is no integrity in this game. Everyone has his or her own interests in mind.

Survivor contestant Ramona Gray was very surprised by who voted her off the show. When she participated in the contest as a castaway on a remote island, she had become a close friend with another contestant, Jenna Lewis. Ramona thought she and Jenna trusted one another and wouldn't vote against each other in the contest. But she was wrong. It was Jenna who cast the deciding vote for Ramona to leave.

Of course, the women were just playing a game, and Jenna tricked Ramona to try to win (which is all a part of playing Survivor*). Had this been a real-life situation and not a game, Jenna would have flunked the trust test. In real life, true friends are trustworthy. They are the same on the inside as they are on the outside.*

Are You for Real?

This next locker holds everything that's real. When something is what it says it is, then it's called **AUTHENTIC.** To earn trust, a leader must be true to what he or she really is like on the inside. A trustworthy leader must be authentic.

I believe in God.

I always try to do what is right.

I believe everyone has something to give.

Authentic

The more authentic you are, the more confidence people place in you, thereby allowing you the privilege of influencing their lives. The less authentic you are, the less confidence people place in you and the more quickly you lose your position of influence.

Take a minute to think about who you really are. What values and beliefs do you have? How can you use them to help out at home, in school, in your church, and in your community?

Now, in your locker notebook, write three words that best describe you.

Suitcases for Kids

When teenager Aubyn Burnside looked inside herself, she found a person who cared a lot about children in foster homes. It bothered Aubyn that when kids moved from foster home to foster home, their belongings were usually moved from place to place in plastic garbage bags. So Aubyn did something about it. She started collecting gently used suitcases to give away to kids in foster care. Over time, Aubyn's idea grew. Before long, she became the leader of a program she created called "Suitcases for Kids." As other young people saw how much Aubyn cared

> PEOPLE DO WHAT
> PEOPLE SEE.

about foster kids, they were influenced to help, too. So far, thousands of suitcases have been collected for foster kids in more than nineteen states across the country.

Climb into the Live-It Locker

You're on your own in this locker. That's because you cannot lead anyone else farther than you have been yourself.

Imagine your swim team has just won the state meet. You and your teammates are so overjoyed that you pick up your swim coach and haul him over to the pool, where you plan to throw him into the water for a celebration dunking. All of a sudden, the coach starts screaming, "No! No! Put me down. I can't swim!" How surprised would you be? Your coach had implied he was a great swimmer. Even though you won the meet, how much trust will you have for your coach now that you have found out he misled you?

Too many times we are so concerned about the end result that we try to take a shortcut to get there. **THERE ARE NO SHORTCUTS WHEN INTEGRITY IS INVOLVED.** Eventually, the truth will come out.

Mirror, Mirror on the Wall

Look in a mirror. That's right. Take a good, long look at yourself.

Did you see your inside on the outside? Did you see someone who is trustworthy, real, and honest? Did you catch a glimpse of some people following you? Were there just a few, or a whole crowd?

To build your life on the foundation of integrity and measure how you're doing as a leader, you can use the following, which was adapted from a poem called "Am I True to Myself?" by Edgar Guest.

> "LIFE IS JUST A MIRROR, AND WHAT YOU SEE OUT THERE, YOU MUST FIRST SEE INSIDE OF YOU."
> —**WALLY "FAMOUS" AMOS,** CREATOR OF A FAMOUS CHOCOLATE CHIP COOKIE RECIPE

> *I have to live with myself, and so I want to be fit*
> *for myself to know.*
> *I want to be able, as days go by, always to look*
> *myself straight in the eye.*
> *I don't want to stand, with the setting sun, and*
> *hate myself for things I have done.*
> *I don't want to keep on a closet shelf a lot of*
> *secrets about myself,*
> *And fool myself, as I come and go, into thinking*
> *that nobody else will know—*
> *The kind of person I really am.*

What Are Your Values and Convictions?

A conviction is a belief or principle that you regularly take action on—one for which you would be willing to die. That's an awesome thought, isn't it? *To believe so firmly in something that you'd die for it.* That's what Rachel Scott did when she answered, "YES, I BELIEVE IN GOD." And that's what Jesus Christ did when He died on the cross for you and for me.

Shell Oil sponsored a poll in which teens were asked to rate the following qualities in order of importance to them (from very important to not important). Some might be equally important, while others were low on the polled teens' list of importance.

65% said being honest was most important.

58% said working hard was most important.

49% said being a good student was most important.

39% said having religious faith was most important.

32% said having lots of friends was most important.

19% said being a great athlete was most important.

18% said having lots of money was most important.

12% said having a boyfriend or girlfriend was most important.

Take a few minutes to think about what things you value in life. What are your convictions? How do they compare with what the teens polled said?

Congratulations!

Can you feel yourself growing as a leader? Are you thinking more often about your values and beliefs? Are you trying to be the same on the outside as you are on the inside? If so, you've taken another step up the leadership ladder. You know you can lead, you have influence, you know how to get things done, and NOW YOU HAVE INTEGRITY! Reward yourself for being totally awesome.

4
Change:
Moving On

Why Should I Change When
Things Are So Cool?

Imagine a world without change. We wouldn't have telephones, CDs, malls, or PCs. The same is true in leadership. Good leaders are always ready to change how they think about things. They know that great ideas come from change and that most of the time change is good.

Have You Seen Henry's Ford?

Henry Ford was the guy who invented the first Ford car, in 1896. The car was very expensive, and only wealthy people could afford one. Then, in 1908, he invented a less expensive car called the "Model T." It was a car that many people could afford. It came in only one color, black, but people didn't care that all the Model Ts looked exactly alike. It was cool just to have a car, because not many people had cars in those days.

It wasn't long, though, before the Model T became old-fashioned. People were bored with the car, and they wanted something that looked different and new. But Henry Ford was a man who loved his car so much that he didn't want to change it. He absolutely **refused to change** even one bolt of the Model T design. In fact, when one of his production men made a new car for Henry to see, Henry got angry. He hated the bright red convertible so much that he tried to tear it apart with his bare hands!

"PEOPLE CAN HAVE THE MODEL T IN ANY COLOR— SO LONG AS IT'S BLACK."
—HENRY FORD, INVENTOR

The only thing that forced Ford to change was that the Model T stopped selling. If Henry hadn't wanted to make money, you probably would never have seen a Ford Mustang, Cougar, or Escort.

Sometimes, it's hard for leaders to change—especially if it means changing something they've built by themselves.

Okay, So I Have to Change What Do I Do Now!?

First learn all you can about change! Consider the story of Joseph.

Genesis, chapters 37–46, tells about Joseph—a young man who was different from Henry Ford in that Joseph wasn't afraid to change.

Joseph was his father's favorite son, and Joseph's ten older brothers were jealous of him. They were so jealous that they sold Joseph into slavery. (Sneaky stuff like that went on all the time in those days.) They took Joseph's coat home to his father, and they said it was all that was left of him. They told their dad that a wild animal had killed their brother.

As the years went by, Joseph went from being a slave to being thrown into prison for doing the

> "EVERYTHING CHANGES BUT CHANGE ITSELF."
> —JOHN F. KENNEDY, THIRTY-FIFTH PRESIDENT OF THE UNITED STATES

right thing. Later he became a great leader in Egypt—quite a change for someone who started out as a shepherd boy. Joseph climbed up the leadership ladder by never resisting change. Instead of asking God, "*Why?*" Joseph asked God, "What do I do now?"

If you want to lead, you have to continue to change, as Joseph did. Once you've learned how hard it can be to change yourself, then you'll understand that it can be just as hard to get your followers to change. Understanding change will be the ultimate test of your leadership skills. But it's a test I know you can pass!

But I Liked It the Old Way!

The word *change* will sometimes give you a weird feeling deep inside your stomach. It's that **"oh-oh!"** feeling that comes with things that are new and different. You probably felt that way when you went from elementary school to middle school.

You knew that some neat things were on the way, but it also felt a little bit scary to be in a new school with different kids. When you feel that way, it's important not to give in to it. Change equals growth, and the more you grow, the better you will lead.

> "WE KNOW THAT IN EVERYTHING GOD WORKS FOR THE GOOD OF THOSE WHO LOVE HIM. THEY ARE THE PEOPLE GOD CALLED, BECAUSE THAT WAS HIS PLAN."
> **—ROMANS 8:28**

Get Out of My Way! I'm Changing

Whoa, wait a minute—changing isn't that easy. First, I have to tell you about some things to watch out for—things that might get in your way. Let's look at the top ten reasons people avoid change.

1. THAT'S NOT WHAT I WANT TO DO.

Imagine that each spring your youth group at church has an end-of-school outing. It's always something different and fun, and something the group decides on together. But this year you have a new leader, and he's already decided you'll go to a ball game. Not everyone wants to go, but the arrangements have already been made. How would you feel if you had nothing to say about it?

When leaders force ideas on followers, the followers might avoid the change. A wise leader allows followers to contribute ideas and to be a part of making decisions.

2. It'll Mess Up How I Do Things!

Think about it. You and your friends love to ride your scooters on the sidewalks in the park. One day, you see signs posted everywhere that say, **"NO SCOOTERS ALLOWED."** Now what are you supposed to do? No one even bothered to ask you what you thought of the idea, and you sure don't like having to change where you ride.

We all have comfortable routines and habits, and people don't like to be told to change the way they do things. Some people avoid change because it makes them think differently and act in ways that are uncomfortable.

> "ALL THINGS MUST CHANGE TO SOMETHING NEW, TO SOMETHING STRANGE."
> —HENRY WADSWORTH LONGFELLOW, POET

3. But What If . . . ?

What if this year you sang a solo at your community's music competition. Your school's choir director thinks you did well, and he suggests that you should compete in a state-level music contest. You're not sure if you should. If you go to state, you'll be competing with young people from lots of different communities, and you're not sure that you're good enough.

Change means trying new things, and that can be scary. Fear makes some people avoid change. How do you react when you're faced with something new? Do you take on the challenge, or do you run from it?

4. I Don't Get It!

Sports are your ticket! You love all of them, especially the ones you can play at school. But yesterday you read in the newspaper that the school board has decided to cut out most of the sports at your school next year. The article talked about budgets, staff cuts, and all sorts of other things you may not have understood. You don't care about their budgets; all you want to do is play sports!

Change is especially hard when you don't understand *why* things have to change. Some people avoid change because they don't understand it.

5. I'm Not Perfect, You Know!

Of course you're not! None of us is. Everybody makes mistakes—even the smartest people in the world.

The worst mistake you can make is to be afraid of making a mistake, because if you don't try new things, you'll never change.

6. But It's Cool the Way It Is . . .

Some people avoid changing because they're satisfied with things the way they are. And then there are people like Jason Jones.

When Jason was a middle school student in Georgia, he noticed children playing around trash dumps, people with problems, and an overall bad attitude in his mobile home park. Did Jason say, "It's cool the way it is"? No, he didn't. Jason decided to change things by setting up a neighborhood committee to provide volunteer services to the park. He helped lead a food drive for needy families, he found tutors for kids with learning problems, and he even helped organize a childcare service. Jason knew change can be good. Instead of sitting back and letting things go on as they were, he *did* something!

7. My Idea Is Better Than Yours!

One day at school, the principal announces that the house of one of your classmates burned down. Nobody was hurt, but everything the family had is gone. The principal asks all of the students to think of ways to help. On the way home from school, you tell your friends of an idea you have to put donation containers in local stores—places where people can drop off clothing and other items. Everyone thinks it's a neat idea until they find out another student is planning a school dance to help raise money. Now everyone is excited about her idea and ignoring yours. How does that make you feel?

It's hard sometimes to change the way you think about someone else's idea, especially if you think your idea is better.

8. Is This Going to Hurt?

"Sticks and stones may break my bones, but change will never hurt me." Okay, so that's not exactly how the saying goes, but it's true.

> "If you don't like something, change it; if you can't change it, change the way you think about it."
>
> —Mary Engelbreit, artist

Whenever things change, you grow. Sometimes you'll win, sometimes you'll lose, and sometimes it won't affect you at all. What's in it for you is the opportunity to become a better leader and a better person.

9. Is Change Worth It?

Some people avoid change unless they know change will result in something better.

Michael Harris, a student in Oklahoma, decided to take a chance. His idea involved getting other people to change—and that's a very hard thing for a leader to do.

Mike was concerned about the environment and the fact that people weren't caring for the earth as they should be. He wanted the earth to be a cleaner place by the time he had kids of his own. So, at age nine, he began recycling. As his ideas grew, so did his projects. He encouraged people to recycle everything from Christmas trees to telephone books. He set up collection sites and increased awareness by presenting programs at schools and writing newspaper articles and doing radio public service announcements. As a result of his efforts, almost half a million people heard his messages about conservation, and more than twenty-two thousand pounds of landfill items were recycled. Mike wasn't afraid to work hard. He knew that if he could get people to change, the change in the environment would be worth it.

What does "worth it" mean to you? What would you like to change?

10. It'll Never Work!

You probably know someone who is always negative, who never thinks anything new will work, who probably whines, and who gives advice such as:

Don't look—you might see.
Don't listen—you might hear.
Don't think—you might learn.
Don't decide—you might be wrong.
Don't walk—you might stumble.
Don't run—you might fall.
Don't live—you might die.
Don't change—you might grow!

Guess what! People like that may not ever change. So don't let them get you down. You and I know that life will always change. Unfortunately, not all change is good, but whenever change happens, be there to meet it with a positive attitude. If something can't be fixed, why waste time on it? Just keep moving forward.

How Can I Change?

Yes, you can! Now that you're aware of the things that can get in your way, you are ready to start changing. If you want to lead, you'll have to change, because a leader has to make personal changes before asking the people who follow him to change.

Think of that game you played when you were a kid—"Follow the Leader." When you were the leader, didn't it feel great knowing that all those kids were doing whatever you did? You believed in your followers, and you trusted them to follow your lead. But what if you'd done something stupid, like led them through a field of poison ivy or over an open manhole? Would your followers have trusted you then?

IT TAKES "CHANGE" TO MAKE CHANGE.

It's wonderful when followers believe in the leader. It's more wonderful when the leader believes in the followers. When everybody believes in everybody else, then there is *trust*. The more the followers trust the leader, the more willing they'll be to accept the leader's changes.

Trust Me!

To earn trust, you have to set a great example. Great leaders not only say what should be done, they walk the talk!

Why do you think the phrase "What Would Jesus Do?" is so popular? It's because the greatest leader of all was Jesus Christ, the Son of God. You can learn a lot about being a leader when you read about Jesus in the Bible. Check out the leadership locker on page 73 to see some of the qualities Jesus had that made so many people follow Him.

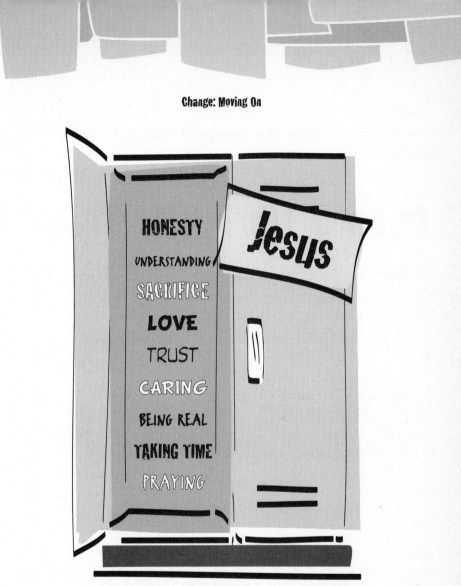

Persuading Followers to Change

Leaders have two characteristics. First, they are going somewhere, and second, they are able to persuade other people to change and go with them. Jesus is a great example of that kind of leader. All of His disciples had jobs or family commitments when they met Him. But Jesus was able to persuade them to change what they were doing to follow Him. Why do you think they were willing to give up so much to make that change?

So, How Do I Get People to Change?

Changing people's habits and how they think is like writing instructions in the snow during a blizzard. The instructions will soon be forgotten, unless everyone is part of the plan.

If your followers think you're awesome, they'll be behind you whenever you turn around. So, how do you convince your followers you're an awesome leader and that you're the one to follow? I can tell you what worked for me.

Honesty

Don't you hate it when people keep secrets from you? You know that something's going on, but you're not a part of it. And you wonder if whatever it is they're keeping from you will affect you. How do secrets make you feel?

A good leader will be honest with her followers about what's going on, and she'll give them time to think about what's going to change. We all need to think about what change will mean to us. Change isn't an easy thing to do, and everyone has to feel it's worth it.

WHEN AND WHY?

Maybe your parents have talked to you about moving your family to California so your dad can take a better job. California! That's clear across the country from where you live. "Hey," you say to yourself, "I don't want to go! I like it right here where my friends are." You wonder when your parents are planning this move. But when you ask them about it, they say something like: "We don't  know for sure yet. We'll let you know as soon as we can." But you worry, because your whole life is about to change! Why don't they tell you when you're moving?

Sometimes leaders don't know the "when" part right away. Your parents are probably just as concerned about a move across the country as you are. Trust them to give you more details when they get them, because good leaders keep their followers informed and share information as soon as they can.

Change Can Be Good

The Metamorphosis

Everyone likes to know how change will affect him. As a leader, you should understand how the changes you are making will affect your followers, and *they* need to know, too.

A leader who knows his stuff will be able to convince his followers that the change will be for the good. Think about the scooter example earlier in this chapter. How would you convince your friends that it's good to find a new place to ride? Maybe you understand that it's dangerous to ride in the park where there are so many other people. You might suggest to your friends that you talk to city officials about creating a safe place to ride. That way, you would be doing something for all of the scooter riders in your community!

Talk about It

Remember that youth leader earlier in the chapter—the one who made plans to go to the ball game without asking anyone first? How might things have been different if he'd asked the group members what they wanted? A ball game is fun, but a trip to an amusement park or an overnight camp-out might be even better.

People like to participate in the decision-making. A good leader will let them do it.

The Good Word Gets Around

On the night I became a Christian, I knew that things were going to have to change for me. The life I lived at high school needed some radical change. I wasn't sure how I or any of my friends would handle it.

I decided that I needed to be honest and upfront with them. I couldn't play any more games. Change has to be met head-on. I immediately told my most talkative friends. I knew they would tell anyone and everyone I couldn't get to! One key student was Jack Martin, a friend from my morning history class. I put a New Testament in my shirt pocket and talked with him until he noticed it. Then—when he saw it, I spoke to him. Word spread. It was the smartest way I could have dealt with the change in my life.

I went on to say no to many opportunities and temptations that followed. I made decisions based on my new set of convictions, and I could do that because I had declared my allegiance.

Put Your Ego in Your Backpack

Imagine you are on a hike through the woods with some friends. One of the guys has been there before, and he says he knows the way. So the rest of you follow him. You don't have a clue where you are, but it's cool, because he knows what's up.

You hike for hours, and you're getting tired. "It's just a little bit farther," your leader says. (Isn't that what he said an hour ago?) Then things start to look familiar. You realize you've been here before. He's been leading you around in circles! Now you're lost, just because this dude was afraid to admit he didn't know where he was going.

A good leader will always admit when he or she is wrong. Watch how fast your followers run if you make a mistake and don't admit it. As I said before, we all make mistakes. If you're afraid of making a mistake, you'll never change. And if you don't change, neither will your followers.

I Believe, I Believe, I Believe!

Richard Hiatt, a middle school student in California, organized a fund-raising walkathon for cancer patients shortly after a friend died of cancer and his friend's sister was diagnosed with leukemia. He asked his school, Scout troops, and other local organizations to help. He also got pledges from businesses and other people throughout his whole community.

Richard's goal was one thousand dollars, but in the end he collected almost fifteen thousand dollars! The money was donated to a local cancer center to help patients pay for medications, checkups, and transportation to and from the hospital.

When he won a Prudential Spirit of the Community Award in 1999, Richard said: "If you really believe in yourself and your cause, others will, too." That's the truth!

When you demonstrate your belief in and commitment to something and show your followers you can make change happen, then your followers will be willing to change along with you.

You're the Greatest!

Don't you love it when someone tells you how great you are? Doesn't it feel good to get rewards and be recognized for the things you do? We all want to feel good about ourselves, and we all need a pat on the back once in a while. As a leader, you expect your followers to tell you they appreciate all of the great and wonderful things you do. But what if that doesn't happen? It might be because you never tell your followers how wonderful they are!

"WHOEVER MAKES HIMSELF GREAT WILL BE MADE HUMBLE. WHOEVER MAKES HIMSELF HUMBLE WILL BE MADE GREAT."
—MATTHEW 23:12

A leader recognizes the needs of followers. A leader helps followers to change. A good leader appreciates the things followers do to help make change happen. And a great leader lets followers know how special and great they are.

Do you ever watch those award shows on television—the ones during which people are honored for being the best in their field? Listen to the speeches they make. From their speeches you can tell the great leaders. It's the people who give most of the credit to their followers. If you're a truly great leader, you'll do that, also.

POP QUIZ

LOOK INSIDE THIS
LOCKER AND SEE
IF YOU KNOW WHAT
THESE THINGS ARE.
YOU CAN'T GUESS
ABOUT WHAT AN
ITEM MIGHT BE.
YOU HAVE TO KNOW
FOR SURE. READY?

Wax lips
Tableside jukebox
Poodle skirt
Party line
Newsreel
P. F. Flyers
Howdy Doody
Gomer Pyle
45 RPMs
The Twist
Hi-Fi
Pet Rock
Beany and Cecil
Skate key
Drive-in
Studebaker
Hula-Hoop
Wiener Whistle
Saddle shoes

How many did you know? There were some pretty strange things in the locker, weren't there? If you had been born fifty years ago, you would have known every one of those things. See if you can find out about the ones you didn't know. A good place to start is by asking your parents or grandparents.

NOW, TAKE THE
QUIZ AGAIN, BUT
THIS TIME, USE THE
LIST IN THIS
LOCKER.

Skittles
Lip gloss
Butterfly clips
E-mail
CNN
Silly String
Sesame Street
CD player
Macarena
Jessica Simpson
Beanie Babies
Furby
Fax machine
Barney
Minivan
Chatter ring
Scooter
Pogs
Air Jordans

Did you do better this time? The second list is different from the first only because people changed. Do you think these changes were for the better? Would you rather be in a poodle skirt playing with a Hula-Hoop, or in jeans playing a computer game?

Change Will Happen, No Matter What

We can't become what we need to be by remaining what we are. Imagine having to go to the bathroom in a shed outside, doing your homework by candlelight, and having to write letters to your friends instead of sending them through E-mail. Think about living without television, radio, computers, microwaves, cars, refrigerators, telephones, CDs, and videos. Your life wouldn't be what it is today if people had remained where they were. Aren't you glad there were leaders who helped people change?

So, how about it? Do you think you understand change? If you do, then you're ready to move on because you've passed the test—the ultimate leadership challenge.

5
How to Get It All Done

I don't know much about ice-skating, but shouldn't you wait 'til the pond freezes?

Bill struggles with the concept of "first things first."

You Can't Get in without a Key

Now that you've passed the ultimate leadership challenge, you're ready to move on to the next step—finding **the leadership key** to unlock your treasure chest. To do this, you must navigate a maze that leads to a key

> "I'D RATHER BE A FAILURE AT SOMETHING THAT I LOVE THAN A SUCCESS IN SOMETHING THAT I DON'T."
>
> —GEORGE BURNS, COMEDIAN

that opens the treasure chest. Along the way, you'll need to decide what to spend your time and energy on, and you'll need to think ahead to grab the key.

Skating on Thin Ice

There are two things that many people find hard to do:

THINKING OF THINGS IN ORDER OF IMPORTANCE, AND DOING THINGS IN ORDER OF IMPORTANCE.

Are you one of those people? If you are, you're in good company. Many well-known people have trouble getting their priorities straight—like champion figure skater Michelle Kwan.

Michelle was only eight years old when she first dreamed of winning the Olympics. At fourteen, she placed eighth at her first world championship competition. A year later, she was sure she'd win a world championship title, but she didn't. Even though she skated a clean program, Michelle thought the judges viewed her as being "a kid," and not the women's figure-skating champion of the world.

During the 1995–96 season, Michelle and her team worked overtime to create her new image. She changed the way she dressed, and she began using makeup to look more grown-up. She even changed her skating style to something more exotic. It worked. In 1996, Michelle won her first world title and United States national title. More titles followed, and Michelle Kwan seemed unbeatable.

But below the surface, Michelle wasn't happy. Inside, she felt nothing but pressure and anxiety, and in 1997 she lost both the national and world competitions. Finally, Michelle admitted to herself what was

> "SET PRIORITIES FOR YOUR GOALS.
> A MAJOR PART OF SUCCESSFUL LIVING LIES
> IN THE ABILITY TO PUT FIRST THINGS
> FIRST . . . THE REASON MOST MAJOR
> GOALS ARE NOT ACHIEVED IS THAT WE SPEND
> OUR TIME DOING SECOND THINGS FIRST."
>
> —ROBERT J. McKAIN, AUTHOR

wrong: Her reason for skating had become for the sake of winning, and not for the love of doing it.

It wasn't until Michelle got her priorities straight, and skated for the love of it, that she began winning again. Michelle Kwan learned to think of things in order of importance and to do things in order of importance. It was more important for her to love what she did than it was for her to win.

Working Smart or Digging Holes?

A good leader knows how to work smart, and a not-so-good leader . . . well, let's just say that a not-so-good leader doesn't have his priorities straight.

Kumar, a middle school student, read that if he worked as hard as he could, he would become rich. The hardest work he knew was digging holes, so he started digging huge holes in his parents' backyard. He didn't get rich—he just got into trouble with his parents!

Okay, so it didn't really happen, but it's a good example of someone working hard, but without priorities. What should Kumar have done? If his goal was getting rich, he should have put some thought into what kind of work would make him a rich man. Then he should have gotten his priorities straight and figured out how to reach that goal.

A good leader thinks of things in order of importance and always works smart.

Anything Goes—No Way!

Many young people live their lives thinking that anything goes. But the truth is that when anything goes—nothing goes. A good leader has to learn to juggle three, four, or sometimes more things at once. And that means setting priorities.

This is where the maze gets tricky. See if you can find your way through by putting things in order.

First Things First

The first things you have to do are the most IMPORTANT things. These are things that can't wait until tomorrow—things like taking out the dog, setting the table for dinner, and learning new music for tonight's choir practice.

Pop music star Jessica Simpson knew to put first things first when she thought about signing on with Sony Music Entertainment. "I was determined that I be able to stay who I am if I signed to a non-Christian music label," Jessica says. And who is Jessica Simpson? She's a focused young singer, a devoted Christian who doesn't smoke, drink, or believe in premarital sex. Jessica's career was about to take a turn, and she had to decide which way to go. Making that decision was an important assignment, and it was one Jessica had to complete right away.

Jessica's top priority was holding on to her Christian values and beliefs. She felt the music she makes would touch the lives of many people, and she was sure she could hold on to her beliefs and still be part of the pop music scene. So Jessica signed on with Sony. "I knew that in pop music I had more of a chance to reach more people," Jessica said. She hopes that fans will see you can be a good person, lead a good life, and still have fun!

Jessica was working smart. She knew she had to put the toughest assignment first—putting her Christian values before advancing her music career.

Remember Jessica when you need to decide what's most important. Ask yourself, "What's the most important thing that I have to do and when must it be done?" The answer is the first thing you should tackle when you set your priorities.

Next Things Next

There will always be things you have to do right away, such as your homework. Then there will be other important things you have a little more time to get done, such as finding a new dress for next week's homecoming dance. The word to remember is DEADLINES. To get through the maze of things that you have to do, you need to be organized. And to be organized, you have to do things on time.

Rosa loved to paint. Everyone in her art class said she was the best. Whatever she did was colorful and bright, and it made you feel good to look at it. The drama coach approached Rosa one day and asked if she'd paint the scenery for the next school play. She had three weeks to do it. "No problem," Rosa said. Three weeks was plenty of time. But then Rosa got busy. She had lots of homework the first week, and the second week she helped her best friend paint a mural on her bedroom wall. On the weekends, she hung out with her friends. By the time the third week came around, **Rosa was in a panic.** She knew the scenery wasn't going to get done on time. As it turned out, the art class had to pitch in to help her. Do you think they thought of Rosa as a leader?

A good leader sets deadlines, and more important—she follows them.

How about you? Do you always do things at the last minute, or do you plan what to do with your time?

Time: Use It or Lose It

When I was growing up, my dad used to give my brother, sister, and me chores to do every week. My list included cleaning up the basement. He never told us how to do our chores unless we asked. He never told us when to do them, either—except that we had to get them all done by noon Saturday. He wanted to teach us to manage our time and not put off important things. If we didn't get them done by noon Saturday, we couldn't participate in the family activities that afternoon.

One Saturday I failed to clean up the basement on time. I had goofed around and procrastinated. That afternoon, my family planned to go on a trip together for the day. I couldn't go with them. I still remember waving to them as they left to go have some fun together. I made up my mind that day—I would learn to prioritize my agenda so that I wouldn't miss out on what I wanted to do. Pay now—play later.

Don't Fret over the Small Stuff

Noah was in charge of his youth group's fund-raising program. He and others in the group went to the homes of church members to collect cans and other things that could be recycled for money. The money they got for the items was going to be donated to the church's Open Pantry—a place where poor people could come to get canned goods and other food. The program was a huge success, and Noah found himself spending all of his time setting up appointments, organizing his workers, and collecting donations. Before long, the church hall was filled with items that had to be taken to the recycling center. Noah felt overwhelmed. *How am I going to get all of this done?* he worried.

What would you do if you were Noah? We'll meet him again in this chapter and find out what he learned and did.

All leaders have to spend their time leading, but good leaders know how to rely on their followers for help. Good leaders learn to ask others for help with smaller jobs so they aren't overwhelmed by the entire project.

Good leaders know not to get tangled up in unimportant things. They know how to **PRIORITIZE.** Some things have to be done **NOW,** some things can **WAIT** until tomorrow, and other things don't have to be done at all.

What Do I Do with the Dregs?

Once you've prioritized the big stuff and found ways to get rid of the small stuff, what's left over? The dregs! The dregs are those little projects that are always hanging around, stuff that you don't know what to do with. The last thing leaders need to worry about is the dregs. You can tackle the dregs little by little each week, or you can ask someone else to help with them. Better yet, use this rule: Before putting off until tomorrow something you can do today, study it. Maybe it's something you won't have to do at all!

Think about your dregs. Is it that stack of teen magazines piled on your bookshelf—the ones you've been meaning to read? Is it that pile of junk under your bed? Or maybe it's those clothes you're not sure whether to keep or give to your little sister. Recycle those magazines, throw away the junk under your bed, and let your little sister pick out the clothes she wants. Then you'll be done with the dregs.

A Locker Filled with Priorities

This leadership locker is about setting priorities. In your locker notebook, write down everything you need to do this week. Then number the items from the most important to the least important. The example in the locker below will get you started.

3. Buy present for Mom

4. Finish history report

1. Study for tomorrow's math test

5. Practice for Friday's concert

2. Call Mike about youth group

Priorities

Choose or Lose

You've just made it through the toughest part of the maze—you've learned about setting priorities. Now you've come to a crossroad. To go on, you have to make a choice. In your locker notebook, complete these statements *honestly*.

1. **You and your friends have talked about volunteering at the local children's hospital. You will:**

    a. try to get the project going
    b. wait for someone to tell you what to do

2. **You've done a totally cool science project for the All-City Science Fair, but it's going to take up a lot of space. You:**

    a. call the organizers and tell them how much space you need
    b. wait until you set up the project and worry about it then

3. **You and three other classmates are assigned to work together on a project. You agree to meet after school. You:**

    a. keep the conversation on track about the project
    b. spend your time talking about school and sports

If you answered "a" to all three questions, you tend to be a leader. If you answered "b," you are most often a follower. Leaders are people who think ahead and get things done. Followers usually wait and react only when they have to. There are times when we are all followers and times when we have to lead. If you always follow, you might want to think about leading once in a while. And if you always lead, you can practice being a better leader.

So, which way will you choose? One way says "leader," the other says "follower." Which road do you think will take you to the key?

The Three "R"s

As you go farther into the maze, you'll see three "R"s. These will keep you going in the right direction. Use them when you're trying to put things in order, and you're more likely to be successful.

"Required"

The first "R" is the one we've all heard many times. It stands for "required." Remember Noah? To solve his problem of too much to do, he first asked himself: *"What is required of me?"* In other words, what do I have to do that no one but me can do? In Noah's situation, it was setting up appointments, organizing his workers, and collecting donations. Take a few minutes to think about what things are required of **YOU**. What things are required at home, at school, and at church? Remember—these are things only *you* can do, things such as being on time and standing up for your values and convictions. Requirements often have to do with rules. Your parents and teachers set some of the requirements for you. Other requirements you set for yourself.

In your locker notebook, write three things that are required of you.

A good leader understands there are some things that only the leader can do and other things that can be done by the followers. A good leader learns to **delegate**, which means **to ask followers for help.**

Share my Christian faith with my friends

Follow the rules Mom and Dad set

Be the best student I can be

Requirements

"Return"

The next "R" is one that will stick with you forever. It's called "return." When you put your best effort into a project, what you get back is your return.

Noah's *return* was knowing that hungry people would have good food to eat.

Return

Tennis great Michael Chang is an example of someone whose effort produces a great return. Michael believes he plays great tennis because of his belief in God. He gives the sport his best effort, not for money or fame, but for God's glory.

At the 1989 French Open, seventeen-year-old Michael shocked everyone by coming from behind to beat the highest-ranked player in the world, Ivan Lendl. No one expected Michael to win, because he was shorter than many of his competitors. But Michael made up for that by using creative strategies. When he won the honor of being the youngest man ever to win a grand slam tournament, *World Tennis* magazine said his performance was "tennis's purest example of intelligence." Michael has his priorities in order, and he plays smart. "Success for me," he says, "is using my talents in the way that God wants me to use them."

Michael Chang's return is the satisfaction of knowing he's doing his very best to touch people in a Christlike way.

Take a minute to think about what gives you the greatest return. What makes you feel great when you give something your best effort? Write about it in your locker notebook.

If you're not getting the return you expect from a certain project, ask yourself: "Am I doing my best at what I do best?"

"Reward"

The last "R" stands for "reward." If you love what you're doing so much that you would gladly do it for nothing, then the great way you feel when you're doing it is your reward. What's fun for you to do? What things make you feel great when you do them? Do you enjoy helping little kids, or old people, or the homeless? Maybe you're great with animals, or writing, or art. Think about how you use your talents to make the world a better place.

Inside your locker notebook write three things that you find rewarding.

Noah
found these
things
to be
rewarding:

Organizing
fund-
raisers

Helping
people in
need

Solving
problems

Reward

GLOW

Becca Laptook of Richardson, Texas, founded a youth volunteer organization called GLOW (Giving and Learning Our Way).

> "YOU CAN'T TRY TO DO THINGS; YOU SIMPLY MUST DO THEM."
>
> —RAY BRADBURY, AUTHOR

"I felt many kids would welcome the chance to be part of a group while having a good time doing things of value for themselves and for others," Becca says. "There are many good teenagers who are happy to help." Becca's group has more than two hundred fifty teen members who volunteer for all kinds of nonprofit organizations, including the local Ronald McDonald House and children's hospital. Their reward is the good feeling they get when they're helping others.

Traps!

Now that you've moved past the three "R"s, you're into the last part of the maze. The leadership key is right around the corner, but first you have to get past some traps.

Trap 1: The Cage

"You can't have it all." How many times have you heard *that* from your parents? Don't they understand it's hard being a teenager? There are so many things you want to do. And there's never enough time to do them all.

Sometimes, you might get a "frozen" feeling when you have too many things going on at once. The next time you feel that way, think of yourself as a caged lion.

Do you know why animal trainers carry a little chair when they go into a lion's cage? It's because the chair is the trainer's most important tool. He holds it by the back and jabs the legs toward the face of the lion. When the poor lion tries to focus on all four legs at once, he can't do it, and a kind of "frozen" feeling comes over him. The lion becomes a wimp because he can't watch all four legs.

YOU CAN'T HAVE IT ALL.

Do you want to be a wimp? Of course you don't! So, whenever you get that frozen feeling—PRIORITIZE! Unfortunately, you may have to give up some things in order to do what's most important.

No. Yes!

When Belinda was asked to lead a little kids' group at her church, she thought she'd say no. But she promised her youth pastor she'd pray about it. Her life was just too busy to add one more thing. She was having a blast learning rock climbing and playing in the school band. She was also getting ready to try out for the soccer and volleyball teams at her school, and during football season she was a cheerleader. With homework, church, family, and friends, Belinda's life was superbusy. So, when her youth pastor asked her to do one more thing, she thought, There's just no way!

But as Belinda prayed about the group, she felt more and more like it was something she wanted to do. She knew she wanted to readjust her priorities and start using more of her time and energy to serve God. So, Belinda made a tough choice. She put trying out for soccer and volleyball on hold, and she said yes to leading the little kids.

Belinda had learned something very important about leadership: All true leaders say no to the good in order to say yes to the best.

What good things are you willing to give up for the best?

Trap 2: The Wrestling Match

Having to make a choice between doing two good things is like a wrestling match. "In this corner," shouts the announcer, "we have Good . . . and in *this* corner we have Best." Good and Best are enemies, and you have to decide who will win. It's easy to decide between Good and Bad, but now what should you do?

As Bob tries pro sumo wrestling for the first time, the importance of step-by-step goal setting becomes apparent.

When you're faced with a decision, ask yourself these questions:

1. **Can somebody else do one of these things?**

2. **Which of these things will bring me, or my group, the greatest return?**

Then pray. If you still can't decide, ask a friend, parent, or teacher for advice; or if you're leading a group, ask your followers which thing they think would be best and why.

Deciding between Good and Best

Your 4-H group has to choose a project. You can either help box candy at a candy factory and bring home lots of free candy or you can help pick peaches. Which choice is best? Wait a minute—you have some points to

> I THINK I CAN, I THINK I COULD.
> I THINK I MAY, I THINK I SHOULD.
> I THINK I MIGHT, I THINK I WILL.
> I THINK I BETTER THINK MORE STILL.

consider. The peaches have to be picked this weekend, or they will spoil and the farmer won't be able to sell them. If you help, the farmer will donate a portion of the peaches your group picks to the charity of your choice, and he will send some fresh peaches home with each of you. On the other hand, the candy factory has agreed to donate to charity a portion of the profits from the candy your group boxes. Think about it. Which choice is best and why? Is there a way to do both?

Hey, you need some more information! So you talk to the candy factory manager and find out the company's offer will be good for anytime during the next three months, while you know the farmer faces a deadline of this weekend for his crop. Still, you and your fellow club members know picking peaches will be hot, hard work, while the candy

ALL TRUE LEADERS SAY NO TO THE GOOD IN ORDER TO SAY YES TO THE BEST.

factory promises sweet rewards. You ask your 4-H adviser for advice. She reminds you that your club is sponsored by the Agriculture Departments, and it would be commendable for the club to help out a local farmer. Together, you and she come up with a decision on which choice is best: Your club will pick the peaches, then have a party after all the work is done! The adviser and several parents will make homemade peach ice cream from the peaches the farmer sends home with each of you. Your club gets two rewards: fresh ice cream and the satisfaction of knowing you helped save a farmer's livelihood. And the candy factory offer still awaits another weekend. One choice was Good, but the other was Best.

Trap 3: The End

Too often we learn too late what's really important. But sometimes, we can turn things around.

Fourteen-year-old Jenny Hungerford from Wisconsin wasted three years of her life hooked on drugs. She ran away from home and caused a lot of worry for her family and her friends. But Jenny refused to give in to her problem! She worked hard to recover, and when she did, she decided to do something that was really important to her—she decided to help other young people stay away from drugs.

Jenny got her priorities straight, and she began giving speeches at schools on the danger of using drugs. She even wrote a four-act play titled *Jenny— A Day in the Life of a Teenage Addict*. Jenny's play got a great response from teenage audiences, and now she's working on pulling together an acting troupe of former teenage drug users. She hopes that together they'll reach even more young people and stop them from taking drugs.

Jenny learned that it's never too late to get your priorities straight. She had taken so much from the people she cared about and from her community. And now, Jenny is giving something back.

Burnout

A lighthouse keeper worked on a rocky stretch of coastline. This was an old lighthouse, and the light was run by oil. The keeper received a new supply of oil once each month to keep the light burning. One night, a lady from the village asked him for some oil to keep her furnace going. Another time, a man asked for some to use in his patio lamp. Another person needed some to lubricate a part in his car. The lighthouse keeper tried to please everyone, so he gave them all the oil they needed. Toward the end of the month, he noticed his supply of oil was very low. Soon it was gone. Before long, the light went out, and several small boats crashed into the rocks.

What did the lighthouse keeper do wrong? He was given the oil for one purpose—to keep the light burning. In trying to do what was good, the lighthouse keeper forgot about what was best.

You Did It!

You did it! You made it through the amazing maze of getting your stuff in order. You've learned all about setting priorities, and working smart, and overcoming the roadblocks that might get in your way. So, what's your reward? The leadership key! This key is the *only* thing that will unlock your success as a leader. It opens a treasure chest that gives you the ability to prioritize things and to work toward positive goals. You're growing as a leader every day. Turn around and take a look. I'll bet there are a lot of people following you now.

6

What to Do
When Problems Come Your Way

Just when you thought everything
was going great...

So, You Got a Problem?

The next step on the leadership ladder is problem-solving. If you're an awesome leader, you'll have a whole team of followers seeking your words of wisdom. (Cool!) They might come to you if they don't know what to do or how to do it, or they might ask your advice when they don't understand *why* something has to be done. You can handle these little problems with no sweat, can't you? But what about the big stuff—what about problems that don't have easy answers?

In Life, As in Math, Positive Is a Plus

I wasn't especially good at solving problems when I was a teenager. I grew in this area during my college years as I saw how quickly I could influence others by helping to solve their problems.

But my first problem-solving lessons came from learning to solve my own problems. I determined I would practice two things. First, I decided to keep a positive attitude. Second, I determined I would obey my mom and dad. I became compliant and decided to go with the flow. Looking back, I feel I was able to prevent many problems due to just those two disciplines: a positive attitude and obedience. It is better to build a fence at the top of the cliff than a hospital at the bottom.

Make Lemonade

There's a world of difference between a person who makes a problem big and a person who has a big problem. Sometimes things happen that can't be fixed—for example, a serious illness, a disability, or losing someone you love. These problems are a tough part of life. But that doesn't mean you have to let them stop you. You can always find a way for problems to lead to something helpful, or maybe even something good.

HEATHER WHITESTONE

Heather Whitestone's problems began when she was eighteen months old and almost died from a bacterial infection. It left her profoundly deaf. Her mother insisted that she learn to speak instead of use sign language. It was a hard thing for Heather to do, and it was six years before she could say her name clearly. While Heather was in her early teens, her parents divorced, which added more trouble to her life. But Heather didn't give up. Her motto all along was "I CAN!" Heather held tight to her strong faith in God, and she refused to allow deafness, peer pressure, or anything else to get in her way. She went to college at Jacksonville State University, where she studied accounting. Then, in 1994, she became Miss Alabama. A year later, Heather Whitestone realized a dream she'd had since she was a little girl—she became the first woman with a disability to be crowned Miss America.

None of her problems stopped Heather from doing her best. **Instead of complaining** about her situation, she became a role model for how hard work and self-esteem can overcome obstacles.

"JIM DANDY" ABBOTT

Baseball was in Jim Abbott's blood. As a little kid, he spent hours bouncing a ball off a brick wall to practice fielding and throwing. He also joined a Little League team and pitched a no-hitter in his first game. He was the star quarterback on his high school football team, a pitcher on his school's baseball team, and he led his intramural basketball league in scoring. Jim even showed enough promise as a high school pitcher to be drafted by the Toronto Blue Jays. He was an ordinary high school jock. . . . Wait a minute. **That's not right** *. . . Jim Abbott was anything but ordinary. He was born with only one hand!*

Jim went to the University of Michigan on a baseball scholarship. As a member of Team USA, he won the U.S. Baseball Federation's Golden Spikes Award as the best amateur player in the country. He pitched in the 1988 Olympics, and from there he played major league ball for the California Angels, the New York Yankees, and the Chicago White Sox. Among his victories was a no-hitter game against the Cleveland Indians.

More Lemonade

ALL OF THESE FAMOUS PEOPLE LEARNED TO SUCCEED— EVEN THOUGH THEY HAVE PHYSICAL PROBLEMS

Marlee Matlin	Actor	Deafness
Itzhak Perlman	Violinist	Polio Paralysis
Marla Runyan	Olympic Runner	Blindness
Mike Utley	Football Player	Spinal Cord Injury Paralysis
Walt Disney	Founder of Disney World	Dyslexia
Stevie Wonder	Singer	Blindness
Albert Einstein	Scientist	Dyslexia
Pope John Paul II	Religious Leader	Parkinson's Disease

A few people told Jim he wouldn't go far in sports, but Jim didn't listen. "I never realized how difficult it would be," he says. "I just always thought it would be possible."

Today, Jim talks to kids who have disabilities, and he works with Little League Baseball's Challenger Division.

What about Your 'Tude?

The way you think about a problem and the way you feel about a problem will help you decide what to do about a problem. Problems are all about attitude. You can face them in a negative or a positive way.

Michael J. Fox is someone else who has a big problem. But he lives with it successfully because of his positive attitude.

Michael J. Fox

Michael J. Fox has been the star of Spin City *and* Family Ties *on TV and several movies, including the popular* Back to the Future *movies. But did you know he suffers from Parkinson's disease? This is a currently incurable disease that destroys the brain cells that control muscle movements. It leaves Michael having to deal with shaking and jerking motions all through his body. What's remarkable is that this disease usually strikes older adults, and it hardly ever affects people as young as Michael.*

The neatest thing about Michael is his positive attitude. He refuses to let his illness get him down. "My life is so filled with positives, and so filled with blessings, and so filled with things that I wouldn't trade for anything in the world," he says. When the doctors told him what was wrong with him, instead of falling to his knees and saying, "Oh, God, this is horrible," Michael said, "Wow. That's not what I was expecting."

Michael left his weekly television series to use his time and positive attitude to help others. He founded the Michael J. Fox Foundation to raise money to research Parkinson's disease. Michael's goal is to find a cure for his illness in less than ten years.

The way that Michael J. Fox feels about his problem and thinks about his problem is leading him to do something about his problem. That's a perfect example of positive thinking.

And then there's Corey Porembski, who has Down syndrome. Does he let that problem stop him from doing the best he can? *NO WAY!*

Corey's Story

Thirteen-year-old Corey Porembski is one of 350,000 Americans with Down syndrome—a condition that slows mental development. But Corey is determined that his disability will not get in the way of his future goals. "My future depends on my education," Corey says. "I want to speak clearly. I want to have a good job when I grow up. I want to have a good life. I want people to see my abilities and what I can do. . . ."

Corey did something about Down syndrome by helping to get one million signatures on a national petition. The petition asked Congress to take action on IDEA (Individuals with Disabilities Education Act). IDEA calls for the federal government to pay 40 percent of the cost of teaching children with educational disabilities.

"I want to make the world a better place for people with disabilities like Down syndrome," Corey says.

There's another positive attitude! In fact, having the right 'tude is such a big part of leadership, there's a whole chapter about it coming up later.

Big Deal!

Everyone you've read about in this chapter has big problems to live with. How are their attitudes different from the guy in chapter 3 who said, "This will never work"? Remember him? Well, *he's ba-a-a-a-ck!* Only now, he's making a big deal out of nothing.

There are many people like the guy in chapter 3. Do you know some of them? Their "problems" aren't their problem. Their problem is that they react negatively to little problems and turn them into big problems.

What really counts is not what happens *to* you but what happens *in* you. Problems can stop you temporarily, but you are the only one who can stop problems permanently.

Just Do It!

There are a lot of problems young people can identify and try to solve. Look around your own community and you might find something that needs to be fixed. That's what Linda Arnade did.

> "AFTER THE VERB 'TO LOVE,' 'TO HELP' IS THE MOST BEAUTIFUL VERB IN THE WORLD."
> —**BERTHA VON SUTTNER,**
> **AUTHOR AND PEACE ACTIVIST**

You Are What You Drink

High school student Linda Arnade discovered a problem while reading an article in her local newspaper—septic tanks in her community were causing groundwater contamination. She was shocked by the idea that people could be drinking contaminated water, so she organized volunteers to help test four hundred wells. The tests showed that wells near septic tanks did have high levels of bacteria. Linda took action and alerted the public to the risk. Her findings were presented to local homeowners and government officials, and as a result, stricter regulations were placed on septic tanks near wells in Linda's community.

Food for Thought

Andrew Leary was doing a school project on hunger in America when he uncovered a problem. He found that hunger wasn't just an issue in other places—it existed in his own neighborhood. To solve the problem, Andrew organized a mass effort to see how widespread the situation was. He did a lot of research and presented his findings to key members of his community. Because of his work, young people and adults joined together to create a permanent soup kitchen to feed the hungry in Andrew's hometown.

Sack It to You

Thirteen-year-old Josh Marcus discovered a problem when he visited a local day-care center for disadvantaged children. These kids desperately needed something that Josh took for granted—backpacks and school supplies. To solve the problem, Josh created a nonprofit corporation called "Sack It to You." His initial effort raised enough money to outfit every child at the day-care center, and more! Josh didn't stop there. He made plans to expand "Sack It to You" to other communities as well.

Now, get out your locker notebook and write three problems you feel you can solve. These can be problems in your community, or problems at school, church, or home. The examples in the leadership locker on page 113 will help get you started.

Problems I
Can Do
Something
About:

My elderly
neighbor's
overgrown
garden

My little
brother's
reading
problem

The need for
volunteers at
our local
Special
Olympics

Problems

Get Your Act Together!

A good test of a leader is his ability to recognize a problem before it becomes an emergency. That means you first have to have a clear idea of what the problem is before you can develop the right action plan. Everyone you've read about in this chapter knew the problem well before anyone acted on a plan. It's important that you—a totally cool leader—learn to do this, too.

Dig at the Roots

A lot of people don't know how to get at the root of a problem. Too many times they attack the symptoms and not the cause.

Pedro woke up one morning with a headache. He took two aspirin, and in a little while the pain was gone. A few hours later, the pain came back worse than before, so Pedro took two more aspirin. Again, the pain went away. This went on for several days until the aspirin no longer helped the pain. "What's the matter with me?" Pedro worried. The pain was so bad now that he hurried to the hospital emergency room. It turns out that he had an infected wisdom tooth.

Do you see that treating the symptoms won't lead to a cure? You have to get at the root of things. To get at the root of a problem, you need to know what questions to ask, whom to ask, and what the important facts are. Then you have to **get involved!**

1. Ask the Right Questions

Think about Linda Arnade and the issue of the septic tanks. If Linda had asked herself a vague question like "What's happening here?" and then gone no further, she might have defined the problem this way:

> Septic tanks in my community are contaminating the groundwater.

Instead, Linda asked herself questions that got to the root of the problem:

Can anyone be harmed by the contaminated groundwater?

How might they be harmed?

Where is the contamination greatest?

Why is it important to find out more about this?

Who can help me find out more?

By answering these questions, Linda was able to get at the root of things and define the problem more clearly:

Septic tanks in my community are contaminating the groundwater. The contaminated water is contaminating wells. When people drink the contaminated water, they might become sick.

The thing to remember is to be specific. Ask questions that answer **WHO, WHAT, WHEN, WHERE, WHY, AND HOW.**

2. Ask the Right People

Here comes that dude from chapter 3 again—the one with a million reasons why something can't be done. Watch out for people like him—those who have an I-know-better attitude. They are often resistant to change, and that can get in the way of getting at the root of a problem.

When you need help defining a problem, *ask the right people.*

Think for a minute about the ultimate problem solver, **Jesus.** He was faced with problems every day—like this one:

Everyone knew about Jesus and the wonderful things He said and did, so there were always a lot of people hanging out with Him. One day, there was a huge crowd of about 5,000. Jesus talked to them, and taught them, and He healed them. This went on all day long, and the crowd was getting hungry. The disciples wanted Jesus to send the people home so they could get something to eat. But Jesus had another idea.

The disciples had five loaves of bread and two fish. "Bring them to Me," Jesus said. Then He told the people to sit down on the grass. He took the five loaves and the two fish, and He looked up to heaven before He started breaking the bread and fish into pieces. (Read that last sentence again.) The neatest thing happened! The bread and fish just kept multiplying. The disciples carried basket after basket of food to the people, and they all had plenty to eat. In fact, when the people were done eating, there was enough left over to fill twelve more baskets.

What did Jesus do to get at the root of the problem? He went to His Father—God. Jesus looked up to heaven, and He asked God for help. The result was enough food for everyone.

When you're looking for the right people to help you understand a problem, don't forget to include God. He's the ultimate authority.

3. GET THE HARD FACTS

Once the facts are clear, the solution to a problem will jump out at you. Listen to what *isn't* being said and gather the important facts.

When Josh Marcus visited the childcare center for disadvantaged children, he wasn't sure what they needed most. He could have relied on what he saw, but instead he dug deeper. He asked questions and gathered information that led to a surprising conclusion. The greatest need wasn't food or clothing or medical care—it was backpacks and school supplies!

Make sure your facts add up. Getting the hard facts will lead you to the right action plan.

4. Get Involved!

Most problems aren't what they first seem to be.

Marta agreed to write a dance routine for her middle school's variety show. On the first day of rehearsal, things went terribly wrong. At one point in the routine, the dancers crashed into each other. "Let's try it again," Marta suggested. The same thing happened.

Marta wasn't sure what was going on, so she decided to take the place of one of the dancers. She tried the routine herself, and right away she realized that the problem wasn't with the dancers, it was with her plan. After making a few small changes, the dance routine worked fine.

Don't just ask the right questions and gather hard facts. Get involved in the process and see where the problems are.

Look on the bright side... Some days are just more exciting.

Get in Line!

It's time now to pull out your leadership key. You need it because a good leader knows to prioritize things when faced with more than one problem. Once you know what the real problems are, you'll have to put them in some kind of order. Never try to solve all of your problems at once—make them line up for you, one by one, in order of importance.

How would you put these problems in order of importance?

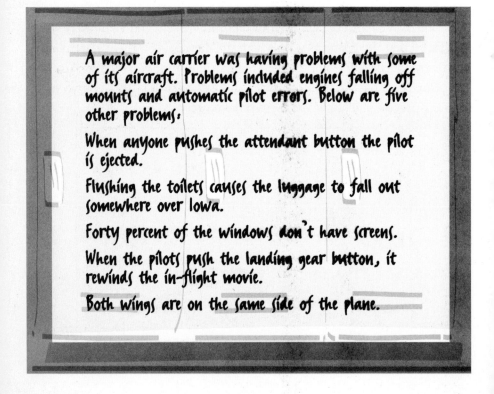

A major air carrier was having problems with some of its aircraft. Problems included engines falling off mounts and automatic pilot errors. Below are five other problems.

When anyone pushes the attendant button the pilot is ejected.

Flushing the toilets causes the luggage to fall out somewhere over Iowa.

Forty percent of the windows don't have screens.

When the pilots push the landing gear button, it rewinds the in-flight movie.

Both wings are on the same side of the plane.

You can't, of course! Why? Because there is one major flaw—the design of the plane! This is just a silly example to show you that prioritizing problems isn't always easy. To solve the little problems, you have to solve the big problems first—in this case, getting a new design for the plane.

Good, Better, Best. A good leader won't just run with a plan that sounds good. A good leader weighs all the possible solutions before deciding what to do. The locker below holds questions that a leader should consider before deciding on the right action plan.

Which solution is more likely to be right?

Which solution will be best for me—or my followers?

(Remember to put your followers' needs first.)

Which solution has the greatest chance for success?

Solutions

List as many solutions to a problem as possible. The more solutions, the better. Most of the time, you'll find that a problem has more than one good solution. Your job, as an awesome leader, is to find the *best* one. Don't throw those other options into your wastebasket, though. If things don't work out, you might need a backup plan.

Hey! Where Did Everybody Go?

A good leader always involves her followers. A good leader is more like a coach than a king. A coach brings out the best in others, helping them to reach deep down inside and discover the best they can be. A king simply gives commands.

Remember King Nebuchadnezzar, from chapter 3? He was the guy who built a gold statue in honor of himself and commanded his followers to bow down to it. If they refused, he threatened to throw them into a fiery furnace. Would you want to follow a leader like him?

Good leaders not only have their followers' best interests in mind, they *INVOLVE* their followers in decision-making and problem-solving. Remember that it's important to make others feel they are a part of the solution.

One Step Higher

So, there you have it—you've just completed a crash course in problem-solving. Every day, you're climbing higher up the leadership ladder. It won't be long, and you'll be at the top.

7
Self-Discipline:
Exercising Your Willpower

When self-control rules.

Get a Grip on Your Life!

Self-discipline, *willpower, self-control*—whatever you call it, it means getting a grip on your life. If you can't lead yourself, you can't lead your followers.

A good leader knows it's important to be **in control of yourself**. That's not always easy. Everyone fights against giving in to some things. It might be

watching television when you have chores to do, hanging out with your friends when there's homework to be done, or chatting on the computer when your room needs cleaning.
If you don't have self-control, you'll give in to *desires*—things that try to pull you away from what you know you should do.

Learning self-control will help you to be an organized and responsible leader. A self-disciplined leader knows how to stay focused and work toward achieving his goals.

> "A PERSON WHO DOES NOT CONTROL HIMSELF IS LIKE A CITY WHOSE WALLS HAVE BEEN BROKEN DOWN."
>
> —PROVERBS 25:28

It Starts with You

Most of us can relate to this sign I saw in an office:

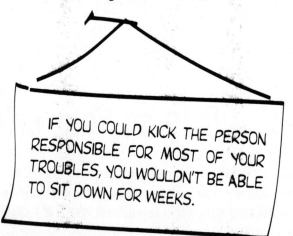

IF YOU COULD KICK THE PERSON RESPONSIBLE FOR MOST OF YOUR TROUBLES, YOU WOULDN'T BE ABLE TO SIT DOWN FOR WEEKS.

> "LOOKING BACK, MY LIFE SEEMS
> TO BE ONE LONG OBSTACLE COURSE,
> WITH ME AS THE CHIEF OBSTACLE."
>
> —JACK PAAR, ENTERTAINER

Is your life out of control? If so, you may be your own worst enemy. That's right. More leaders fail because of inner issues than outer ones. Take a look inside yourself. Maybe you're not as good as you can be because some areas of your life are out of control.

LEANN'S COUCH-POTATO BLUES

Leann thought there were three levels of fitness: athletes, people who play games for fun, and COUCH POTATOES. She fit into the last category. Leann was uncoordinated when it came to sports, and gym class was torture for her. It wasn't a lesson in fitness; it was public humiliation. So, rather than face her problem, Leann gave up. She settled in with a bag of chips and accepted life as a couch potato.

Months went by, and Leann's grade in gym dropped to a D. To pass gym, she needed to run fifty yards in a certain amount of time. There was no way Leann could do it in the shape she was in. But if she didn't do it, she'd have to take gym in summer school.

So, Leann started training. First, she did some jumping jacks and lifted five-pound weights. Then she walked. Then she ran. Before long, Leann felt great! She actually enjoyed exercising . . . and she passed the fifty-yard test with no problem at all. And Leann kept on running. Today, she enjoys running in marathons!

Sometimes self-discipline becomes the choice of achieving what you really want by doing things you don't want to do.

"GOD DID NOT GIVE US A SPIRIT THAT MAKES US AFRAID. HE GAVE US A SPIRIT OF POWER AND LOVE AND SELF-CONTROL."

—2 TIMOTHY 1:7

What Are You Waiting For?

Excuse me...I think he's on a mission!

Seeing his goal clearly within reach, Sparky pursued his dream with a passion.

"Today is the first day of the rest of your life." You've probably heard that a hundred times, but it's true. Today is as good as any to start practicing self-control. If you don't start now, you may never start. You

"YESTERDAY I WAS A DOG. TODAY I'M A DOG. TOMORROW I'LL PROBABLY STILL BE A DOG. SIGH!"

—SNOOPY IN "PEANUTS" COMIC STRIP
BY CHARLES M. SCHULZ

could end up like Charlie Brown! He once said his life was mixed up because he missed all the rehearsals. In other words: YOU HAVE TO START PREPARING FOR TOMORROW BY WHAT YOU DO TODAY.

I wonder if Einstein got
started this way?

Little by Little

You're working hard at getting a grip on your life. But you don't have to do it all at once. You'll learn more about self-discipline if you take it in *small steps*.

Astronaut Neil Armstrong was the first man to walk on the moon. When he set foot on the moon's surface, he said, "That's one small step for man, one giant leap for mankind." The space program is an example of how small steps lead to something big. First, unmanned rockets were sent up, then monkeys were sent into space to see if it was a safe place for man to be; next, men orbited the earth in space capsules; finally, men walked on the moon. Great things take time—they don't happen overnight.

Pull out your leadership notebook and list three things in your life that you want to improve. Place them in order of importance. You should tackle them one at a time. See the locker on page 127.

Get It Together!

Being **organized** is an important part of being self-disciplined. Can you imagine Britney Spears going out on stage not knowing which songs she's going to perform? Or what if Jonathan Taylor Thomas didn't know his lines when he showed up on the set of *Home Improvement*? Jonathan and Britney are organized. They have their priorities straight, and they don't let other things get in the way of what they have to do—that's why they're leaders in their field.

When you're disorganized, your followers might not see you as a good leader. But when you're organized, it's like you have a special power. You walk with a sense of purpose, your priorities are clear in your mind, and

Things I'd Like to Improve:

I want to get along better with my sister.

I want to get better grades in school.

I want to always be on time.

Improvement

you do complicated things in a way that makes them look easy. When you're organized, people believe your promises because you always follow through. Things fall into place when you take action on your plans. You move smoothly from one project to the next without wasting any time, and best of all—PEOPLE FOLLOW YOU!

The Map to Organization

1. Set Your Priorities

There's that word again—**PRIORITIES.** Prioritizing is simply arranging things in order of importance, and not only arranging them, but also being *committed* to them. It sounds easy enough to do, but sometimes setting priorities is hard. There's always something else you could or should be doing.

Teens today face tough choices. But if you look around you, you'll

JAMAL AND MARTINA

Jamal, a sixth-grade student, worries about what his friends will think if he turns down a camping trip to stay home and study for exams. All through elementary school, Jamal was a straight-A student. Grades are important to him, but now there's peer pressure to deal with. It's more cool to hang out with friends than to do homework.

Martina worries, too, because there's too much to do. She's involved in soccer, her church choir, student council, French club, and she volunteers at the humane society two evenings a week. Martina often feels stressed-out. But if she gives up any of her activities, it would mean not seeing her friends as often—and, she quietly fears, maybe not being as popular.

notice that **teens who are real leaders have their act together.** Jamal and Martina are both good leaders. Jamal decided that if he skipped his favorite television shows the week before the camping trip and studied instead, he would be prepared for the exam, *and* he would have time to go camping. And Martina reluctantly gave up French club so she would feel less stressed-out. These decisions weren't easy for Jamal and Martina, but they did what they had to do to keep their lives in control.

We're all **overwhelmed** sometimes. But being organized helps avoid being overwhelmed. When you're organized, you know what you need to do. You prioritize things in order of importance. You do projects one at a time.

2. Develop Systems That Work for You

Organization helps leaders stay on time and not forget things. It might help you get organized if you write things down and mark important dates on a calendar. Systems—like to-do lists, Internet search engines, and word processing software—are your tools. Make them work for you. They can help you to do things better and they'll save you time.

3. Expect the Unexpected

How many times have you planned to do something outdoors, and it rained? Or maybe you were in the middle of watching a totally awesome adventure movie, and a friend called to ask you to go to the mall. And what about those times when you opened the freezer expecting to find ice cream, and you found that your little brother got there first?

LIFE IS FILLED WITH SURPRISES. An organized leader expects the unexpected and is ready to deal with it. Sometimes that means changing plans. Other times, it means allowing more time to get things done.

4. Organize Your Workspace

Imagine a world with no computers! No scanners! No CDs, VCRs, DVDs, or video games! Guess what? That was your parents' world as children. Spies in the 1940s had less-sophisticated gear than most students have today. Did you know that your parents had to hand-write their assignments or type them on a typewriter? Do you even *have* a typewriter at home? And storage—that was a folder stuffed with paper and stuck in a drawer. Think about it. Is that how you want to live?

Today's technology makes it easy for you to be organized if you learn to use all the tools provided. So there's no excuse for a messy workspace. **A GOOD LEADER WORKS SMART,** and that means being able to quickly find things when they're needed.

5. Focus on Results, Not the Activity

An organized leader keeps her eyes on the end result. She does the right thing by making sure things are done right. She sets priorities and never loses sight of what's most important.

Responsibility = Work

LEADERS WHO ARE SELF-DISCIPLINED ARE RESPONSIBLE LEADERS. They are accountable not only for what their followers do, but also for what they do themselves.

Jesus said, "Everyone who has been given much will be responsible for much. Much more will be expected from the one who has been given

BROOKE

Brooke learned that the school's advisory council was considering cutting funds for her school's cooking club, so she decided to do something about it. She got permission from her teacher to organize a special dinner for advisory members, so they could get a clearer idea of what the club did—and, she hoped, so they would decide to keep it.

Her teacher gave her a list of the names and addresses of the members, and Brooke went to work. She met with the cooking club, and together they planned the menu and designed the invitations. There would be a lot to do in a short time, but in the end, Brooke believed it would be worth it.

The day of the dinner arrived, and everyone was busy. The tables were set, the place cards were in place, and the school kitchen was filled with wonderful smells. But when dinnertime came, only a few people showed up. Did they all forget? No. Brooke was so busy planning the dinner that she forgot to send out the invitations until three days before the event. By that time, most of the advisory members had other plans for the evening.

What might Brooke have done when she noticed her mistake? Before mailing the invitations, she could have called the advisory members and asked if they would be able to come. Or she could have admitted her mistake to the cooking club and rescheduled the dinner.

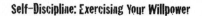

Be
Responsible:

For who
you are

For what
you can
do

For what
you have
received

To those
you lead

Responsibility

more" (Luke 12:48). Think about that for a minute. When you are a leader, you are expected to do a lot more than your followers do. You have responsibility, and it's your job to do the right things—and to do them right.

Look inside the leadership locker on page 132. It holds four steps toward becoming more responsible.

It's Not My Fault!

Brad was baby-sitting the neighbor kids. He was outside playing ball with them when it began to get cold. He went inside to get some warm sweaters, when all of a sudden he heard a crash! He rushed to the living room and saw glass all over the floor. The window was broken, and the ball was on the carpet. *It's not my fault,* Brad thought.

What's up with Brad's attitude? He was the baby-sitter that day, and he was the one in charge. Was it right for Brad to make excuses, or should he be accountable for the broken window? Guess what? He *is* responsible for that broken window. He left the kids alone

TAKE RESPONSIBILITY FOR WHO YOU ARE.

outside, and a good baby-sitter knows not to do that. He should have brought them in to get their jackets. And once the window was broken, it was Brad's responsibility to clean up the glass so the children wouldn't get hurt.

The first step toward being a responsible leader is taking responsibility for who you are.

I Don't Wanna!

Kellie's church was hosting a party for all the Christian youth groups in her community. There was a lot of fun stuff to plan, but Kellie got stuck with a crummy job. She was asked to clean up the church hall for the party. That meant doing things like washing the floor and cleaning the windows. "I don't wanna do this," Kellie said to herself. She decided to do it as quickly as possible, so she could move on to something more fun. Kellie's pastor was disappointed when he saw the job she did. There were streaks on the windows and spots on the floor.

TAKE RESPONSIBILITY FOR WHAT YOU CAN DO.

Have you ever left a place because it was dirty? Or maybe you didn't eat something because it was prepared in a place that didn't look clean? How do you think the youth group members will remember their visit to Kellie's church? You may not notice a clean room, but you *do* notice a dirty one. Kellie's job wasn't glamorous, but it was important. Maybe she could have listened to her favorite CD while she worked to make the job less boring, or maybe she could have asked the pastor if two people could do the job so there would be some company.

Responsibility means doing what you can do, and doing it as well as you can—even if you're not the leader.

Don't Forget to Look behind You

Some years ago, Coach Bo Schembechler's Michigan Wolverines were playing Texas A&M, and they couldn't move the football. All of a sudden, Dan Dierdorf, their offensive lineman—who was probably the best in the country at that time—came rushing over to the sidelines. Fed up with the team's performance, he yelled at the coach, in front of everybody on the sidelines, "Listen, Coach! Run every play over me! Over me! Every play!" The coach listened to the lineman, and that's just what they did. Michigan ran off-tackle six times in a row and marched right down the field to win.

When the game is on the line, great leaders always take responsibility for leading their teams to victory.

Me? A Role Model?

Here comes another familiar word: INTEGRITY—you might remember it as leadership's most important ingredient. Does integrity fit into the idea of self-discipline? It sure does, because integrity makes you accountable to your followers. **When you act with integrity, you are being a good role model.**

Integrity needs self-discipline. People with integrity are the same on the inside as they are on the outside. They do what's right, and they are able to keep focused on their goals. They have nothing to hide—their lives are open books. Followers respect leaders with integrity.

I will
live what I teach,

do what I say,

be honest with others,

put what is best for others ahead of what is best for me.

Role Model

Look inside the leadership locker on page 136 for the secrets to being a good role model—one with integrity.

Living What You Teach

You are probably already thinking about what you want to do when you graduate from high school. But have you thought a lot about what you want to *be*? Deciding what to be is more important than deciding what to do. Your character—the kind of person you are—will determine what kind of leader you will be in whatever career you choose.

Doing What You Say

Demetrius was involved in a walkathon to raise money for a classmate who was very ill with cancer. Each walker promised to get a certain number of sponsors, and each sponsor would sign a pledge card promising to contribute ten dollars if the walker completed the twenty-mile walk. Everyone was shocked when Demetrius promised to get five hundred sponsors. "No way!" his classmates said, but Demetrius was a young man of integrity—when he made a promise, he kept his word. How did he do it? Demetrius asked the basketball coach at the local college if he could make an announcement about the walkathon at the start of the next home game and distribute pledge cards. The coach agreed. Fifteen hundred people were in the stands that night, and more than five hundred of them signed the pledge cards that Demetrius distributed during the game. True to his word, Demetrius completed the walk, and his sponsors contributed more than five thousand dollars toward his classmate's fund.

What would have happened if Demetrius had just "talked big" and not followed through? Doing what you say you will do takes self-discipline. If you're not sure you can do something, don't promise it.

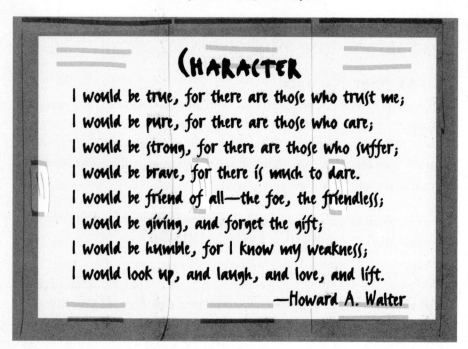

CHARACTER

I would be true, for there are those who trust me;
I would be pure, for there are those who care;
I would be strong, for there are those who suffer;
I would be brave, for there is much to dare.
I would be friend of all—the foe, the friendless;
I would be giving, and forget the gift;
I would be humble, for I know my weakness;
I would look up, and laugh, and love, and lift.

—Howard A. Walter

BEING HONEST WITH OTHERS

Sometimes it's hard to fight the desire to be dishonest. Most of us are honest about big things, but it's the little stuff that gives us trouble. Watch out for that inner voice that tells you, *It wasn't your fault, nobody will know, it's just a little thing, it's okay to lie about it—just this once. You won't get caught.* That's *desire* talking, and you don't want to listen.

BEING HONEST MEANS YOU HAVE INTEGRITY. If you're dishonest—even once—you will lose followers. Nobody trusts a liar. And who wants a liar as a role model?

CARLTON

Fourteen-year-old Carlton and his older brother didn't know what they were getting into when they took a drive to see family on New Year's Day. The dark clouds and heavy downpour made it hard to see where they were going. Soon, the roads became flooded, and it was almost impossible to travel. That's when Carlton's brother made a terrible mistake—he kept going. Before long, the floodwaters forced the car off the road and into a deep, water-filled culvert. Immediately, water began to rush into the car, and in no time the car was submerged. Carlton got out, but his brother didn't.

"I didn't even think before I did what I did," Carlton said. "I dove under water, and I used my hands to break the sunroof. I got my brother out of the seat belt, and I pulled him out of the car."

Putting Others First

Carlton risked his own life to save the life of his brother. By doing so he showed the mark of a true leader: putting others first. Desire might tell you to do what's best for you, but *integrity* and *self-discipline* will always tell you to PUT OTHERS FIRST.

Turn On the Faucet

Now that you know all about self-discipline, you should start practicing it right away—**no matter what.** Think of it this way: The water doesn't flow until the faucet is turned on. As you become more disciplined, you'll see yourself growing as a leader. You'll get organized, you'll be responsible, you'll act with integrity, and you'll have a whole crowd of people wanting to follow in your footsteps.

> "THIS IS MY COMMAND: LOVE EACH OTHER AS I HAVE LOVED YOU. THE GREATEST LOVE A PERSON CAN SHOW IS TO DIE FOR HIS FRIENDS."
> **—JOHN 15:12-13**

8
What's Your Attitude?

For Sale!
VINEGAR FLY TRAPS
Draws flies like magic

Get Yours Now!!
While supplies last!
(stock options available)

A business venture that just didn't fly.

Honey, Vinegar, and Flies

Tia and her mom went Christmas shopping at the mall. As soon as they got there, Tia's mom was miserable. So much for Christmas spirit. The place was crowded with noisy people, and it was hard to get into the stores, let alone buy anything. At noon, they went to Tia's favorite restaurant for lunch, and they had to wait an hour to be seated. While they were waiting, Tia noticed her mom looked tired. She said her feet hurt—and that was about all she said. She was in a very grumpy mood.

When they left the mall that afternoon, they passed a security guard standing by the exit. "Did you see the nasty look that guy gave me?" Tia's mom asked. Tia couldn't keep still any longer. "He didn't give it to you, Mom," she said. "You had it when you went in."

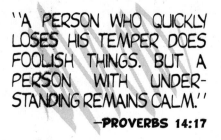

"A PERSON WHO QUICKLY LOSES HIS TEMPER DOES FOOLISH THINGS. BUT A PERSON WITH UNDER-STANDING REMAINS CALM."
—PROVERBS 14:17

The moral of the story is: A spoonful of honey will catch more flies than a gallon of vinegar. In other words, how people react to you has everything to do with your 'tude. A good one brings people in; a bad one pushes people away.

No matter how well you think you can hide a bad attitude, others know all about it. It's in the way you walk and the way you talk, and it shows on your face!

Attitude Is Where It's At

Attitude is more important than appearance, talent, or skill. It's more important than the past, the future, money, circumstances, failures, or successes. It's even more important than what other people think about you, or say about you, or do to you. The awesome thing about attitude is that you're always in charge of it. Every day it's up to you to decide what kind of attitude you're going to have.

Caleb and the Promised Land

God had delivered the Israelites from slavery in Egypt, and now it was time for them to enter a place God called the Promised Land. The Israelites knew they would have to fight some pretty tough dudes before they could enter, so they sent spies on a mission into the Promised Land to see what was up. Caleb was one of those spies.

When the spies returned, the Israelites had a sort of town-hall meeting so the spies could tell the people what they saw. One spy said, "The people there are very strong. They won't leave without a fight—" "It won't be easy," another spy interrupted. "There are big cities that are well guarded." A third spy chimed in, "And that's not the worst of it. Some of them are like giants! We're as small as grasshoppers compared to them."

In the middle of all this, Caleb stood up, and he told everyone to be quiet and listen. When he had the floor he said, "We should go up and take the land for ourselves. I know we can do it!"

Can you imagine the reaction of the other spies? Why do you think Caleb was so positive while everyone else was so negative?

> **"THE LONGER I LIVE, THE MORE I REALIZE THE IMPACT OF ATTITUDE ON LIFE."**
>
> —CHUCK SWINDOLL, CHRISTIAN LEADER

Attitude makes all the difference in leading others. The attitude of a leader is important because it will influence the way followers think and feel. Great leaders understand the right attitude will set the right atmosphere, which enables the right response from followers.

Your 'Tude Belongs to You

You own your attitude, no one else's. It's all yours. You make it. And it's the most valuable thing you own. Without a good attitude, you'll never be all that you can be. Your attitude determines what you see and how you handle your feelings.

Do You See What I See?

A man who couldn't find his best saw suspected that his neighbor's teenage son, who built soapbox racers, had stolen it. During the next week everything the teenager did looked suspicious—the way he walked, the tone of his voice,

his gestures. But when the man found the saw behind his own workbench, where he had accidentally knocked it, he no longer saw anything at all suspicious about his neighbor's son.

Expectations have a great deal to do with attitude. What you expect may be totally false, but it will determine what kind of 'tude you have.

Rule Your Emotions!

Your attitude determines how you handle your emotions. Notice I didn't say your attitude determines *how you feel*. There's a big difference between how you feel and how you handle your feelings. Everyone has times when he or she feels bad. Your attitude can't stop your feelings, but it can keep your feelings from stopping you. Unfortunately, too many people allow their feelings to control them until they end up like poor Ziggy in the comic strip.

''THE ONLY DISABILITY IN LIFE IS A BAD ATTITUDE.''
—SCOTT HAMILTON,
OLYMPIC
FIGURE SKATER

He's sitting beneath a tree, gazing at the moon, and he says, "I've been here and I've been there. I've been up and I've been down. I've been in and I've been out. I've been around and I've been about. But not once, not even once, have I ever been 'WHERE IT'S AT'!''

Cody Unser

Cody Unser, daughter of racecar driver "Little Al" Unser, was an eighth-grade student in Albuquerque, New Mexico, in 1999 when she was struck suddenly by a rare spinal cord disease called transverse myelitis, or TM. The illness left her paralyzed from the waist down and in a wheelchair. Even though things are sometimes tough for Cody, she handles her emotions in a positive way. "I decided to take a negative experience and turn it into a positive to help others—and me," Cody said.

Cody founded the Cody Unser First Step Foundation to promote public awareness of TM and, she hopes, to find a cure for it and other forms of paralysis. The story of her positive attitude has been told in People *magazine and on the CBS television show* 48 Hours. *"I've learned how important hope is," Cody says, "and to never give up."*

Adjust Your Sails

The pessimist complains about the wind. The optimist expects it to change. The leader adjusts the sails.

A Leadership Locker with Attitude

Get out that leadership notebook and write the name of someone whom you greatly admire. Then write two things that you admire most about that person. See the locker on page 147.

Most likely, the things you admire about this person have to do with attitude.

A Bad 'Tude Gets You Nowhere

Once your mind is **"TATTOOED"** with negative thinking, your chances for success diminish.

Arnold Palmer, a great professional, title-winning golfer, has a wonderful attitude.

There's a plaque on a wall in his home that tells why he has been successful on and off the golf course. It reads as boxed on page 148.

What's the difference between a golfer who wins one golf tournament and a golfer such as Arnold Palmer, who won tons of tournaments? Is it

> If you think you are beaten, you are.
>
> If you think you dare not, you don't.
>
> If you'd like to win but think you can't,
>
> It's almost certain you won't.
>
> Life's battles don't always go
>
> To the stronger or faster man,
>
> But sooner or later, the man who wins
>
> Is the man who thinks he can.

ability or luck? No way! When an average of less than two strokes per tournament separates the top twenty-five golfers in the world, the difference has to be something more than ability or luck. It's attitude that makes all the difference.

People with negative thinking may start well, have a few good days, and win a match. But sooner or later (it's usually sooner), their attitudes will pull them down.

Hello? Are You in There?

Too many people believe happiness is a condition. When things are going great, they're happy. When things are going bad, they're sad. Some think happiness can be found by being someone famous or by being in a certain place. Others think happiness comes from knowing or being with a particular person.

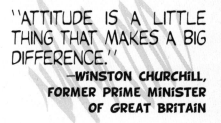

"ATTITUDE IS A LITTLE THING THAT MAKES A BIG DIFFERENCE."

—WINSTON CHURCHILL, FORMER PRIME MINISTER OF GREAT BRITAIN

The thing to remember is that **God chooses what we go through. We choose how we go through it.**

Take a look inside yourself. Come on, now—look really hard. Who's in there? Will you find someone who sees the glass as half empty, or someone who sees it as half full?

Is Your Attitude Contagious?

LEADERSHIP IS INFLUENCE. People catch our attitudes just like they catch our colds.

Think about it. If your attitude is contagious and if you have lots of followers, they will catch your 'tude. If you smile, you'll get lots of smiles in return. If you frown, then that's what you'll get—frowns and a lot of grumpy followers.

Who says you're not tougher, smarter, better, more hard-working, and more able than your competition? It doesn't matter if they say you can't do it. What matters—THE ONLY THING THAT MATTERS—IS YOUR ATTITUDE.

JACKIE JOYNER-KERSEE

When Jackie Joyner-Kersee was fourteen she watched the 1976 Olympics on television. Little did she know that God would literally ask her to "run the race that is before us and never give up" (Hebrews 12:1). Jackie would become a six-time Olympic medalist in track and field and a woman who's been described as "the greatest athlete in the world."

What makes Jackie a great leader is her attitude. "I want to give people the courage and determination to realize they can change their life," Jackie says.

She grew up in a tough neighborhood, and she had plenty of opportunities to make the wrong choices. But instead Jackie chose to be involved in her church and to participate in sports at a local community center.

Becoming a great athlete took a lot of self-discipline, and Jackie was often hard on herself. But she tried not to let her success change her. "Sometimes people who succeed get an attitude," she says. "I try not to let my athletic accomplishments change who I am inside."

Jackie Joyner-Kersee is a great example of someone with a contagious attitude. Today, Jackie spends much of her time helping young people. Recently, she founded the Jackie Joyner-Kersee Youth Center in her hometown of East St. Louis, Illinois.

A Stinky Leadership Locker

This leadership locker is like a locker that holds dirty socks and sweaty gym clothes. It stinks! It stinks because it has a bad attitude.

Take a minute to look inside you and see if anything gloomy is lurking. Then, in your locker notebook, write down three negative attitudes that you feel could have a bad influence on your family and friends.

Sometimes I'm impatient.

I don't always do what I say I will.

I complain a lot.

Bad Attitude

Does Your Attitude Need an Overhaul?

So maybe you found a few things in there that you weren't too happy about. Not to worry. It's not the end of the world. Your attitude is something you *can* change. Do you want to know how? Try this.

Five Steps to a New You

1. Identify Problem Emotions

Hey, guess what! You've done this step already. When you looked inside you and found some bad 'tudes, you were identifying *problem emotions.* This is the stuff you want to get rid of, because it will keep you from becoming a totally cool leader.

2. IDENTIFY PROBLEM BEHAVIORS

Tomas is always spreading doom and gloom wherever he goes. If someone has an idea, Tomas is sure to dislike it and say so loudly. Wanna see him run real fast? Try to get him involved in volunteering for something. Tomas has a million excuses for why things shouldn't be done.

Do you know someone like Tomas? There are a lot of people like him out there. Hopefully, you're not one of them. Tomas probably acts as he does because he has low self-esteem. It's easier for him to have a negative attitude than to get involved and face the risk of failing.

It's important to try to discover which emotions trigger problem behaviors. What things trigger your negative emotions?

3. IDENTIFY PROBLEM THINKING

Willie lives in the "projects" in Chicago. When he was only nine, he saw someone murdered in front of his house. Two years later, his older brother was shot and killed in a gang war. Then, when Willie was thirteen, his mother died of cancer, and Willie began to get into trouble. By

> "ALWAYS LOOK AT WHAT YOU HAVE LEFT. NEVER LOOK AT WHAT YOU HAVE LOST."
> —ROBERT H. SCHULLER, CHRISTIAN LEADER

the time Willie and his brothers and sister went to live with their grandmother, Willie had been arrested several times.

Willie isn't a bad person. He's just convinced himself that he won't amount to much. He dwells on where he is and on what he's lost, instead of looking toward where he can go and what he can accomplish. It's easy to get caught up in Willie's kind of thinking, especially when you've been through hard times.

Do you see any of Willie's thinking inside you? Do you feel stuck in any way? Maybe you think you're too fat, too thin, too tall, or too short to do the things you want to do. Maybe you have a disability you think holds you back. (Do you see all the doors and windows inside you? If one doesn't open, what do you do? You could stand and knock on it and wait forever for someone to open it for you, or you could explore those other doors and windows. One might open to your future.) Look at the choices you have in life. If Willie had managed to find something—ANYTHING—good to be involved in and look forward to, he could have turned his life around.

The first step to getting rid of problem thinking is to be aware of it. This week, pay special attention to the things you do and say. See what's lurking, and chase it away with a positive 'tude.

4. Identify Right Thinking

Marcus Houston, a high school student in Colorado, is a great example of someone who is "right thinking." Marcus was concerned about middle school students in his school district who were ineligible for sports because of poor grades or behavior problems. Because he was an excellent student and a football star, Marcus wanted to find a way to help.

What did he do? He created an educational program called "Just Say Know." Marcus looked inside himself and gave some thought to how he had become a leader in his school. Then he put together a presentation on how he gained success, and he went to middle schools to talk to the students.

Marcus tells them that how they dress, talk, and act reflects their attitudes and often influences teachers in either a positive or negative way. "Reach for opportunities instead of excuses," Marcus says. "Success is not an accident. It's something you work hard to achieve."

Working hard means looking inside, seeing what's there, and changing any problem thinking to right thinking.

5. Walk the Talk

Right now, wherever you are, make this promise to yourself:

> Wherever I go and whatever I do, I will practice right thinking and show others nothing but a good and positive attitude.

If you keep that promise, you'll attract many followers.

Put Your Thinking in a Frame

Think of these words:

I CAN'T.

I WON'T.

I'M NOT.

What kind of picture do these words paint in your mind? Inside your locker notebook, describe the painting.

Now, think of these words:

I CAN.

I WILL.

I AM.

What kind of picture do these words paint in your mind? Inside your locker notebook, describe the painting.

Do you see the difference? If you don't like your attitude, you can always change the picture. Reframing your attitude means: I may not be able to change the world I see around me, but *I can change the way I see the world within me.*

Think Like Nike

As you begin to change your thinking, start immediately to change your behavior. Act the part of the person you would like to become. Take action on the behavior you admire by making it *your* behavior. Too many people want to feel, then take action. That doesn't work.

Think like the Nike ads—**Just do it!** Volunteer to help someone, join a club, make some new friends. After you start doing the thing, that's when the motivation comes and makes it easy for you to keep on doing it. Whatever it is you know you should do, *just do it.*

Practice Makes Perfect

An action repeated becomes an attitude realized. Practice a new attitude about something over and over every day and watch your life change for the better.

One day, I was asked to put together a simple plan to help a young person change some wrong attitudes. I recommended two things. The first of which is in the box on page 159.

The second thing I told her to do was to do the first thing every day, not just once or only when she felt like it, but as often as she could.

Practice this advice, and WATCH YOUR LIFE START CHANGING!

SAY THE RIGHT WORDS,
READ THE RIGHT BOOKS,
LISTEN TO THE RIGHT CDs,
BE WITH THE RIGHT PEOPLE,
DO THE RIGHT THINGS,
PRAY THE RIGHT PRAYER.

Life Is an Attitude

When he was in high school, Ron Heagy hoped to make a career in pro football. That was before he was paralyzed in a diving accident that left him a quadriplegic. Ron felt like giving up on life, until he received what he believed to be a message from God. Ron then realized he had potential—he just had the wrong attitude! Ron changed his thinking. He learned to write by holding a pen in his mouth, type on a computer keyboard by using a pointer clenched between his teeth, and to paint by holding a brush in his mouth. He went to college, where he earned a master's degree in social work and graduated summa cum laude.

Ron faced a lot of frustration as he looked for a job, but he didn't give up. He and his wife, Christy, decided to start a not-for-profit business called Life's an Attitude.

As a part of his work, Ron travels the country encouraging people to have a good attitude and use their potential. He even started "Camp Attitude," a camp for people with disabilities.

In spite of all the bad things that happened to him, Ron believes it's really true that "in everything God works for the good of those who love him" (Romans 8:28).

Ron is living proof that a positive attitude can replace a negative one. And, oh, what a change it makes!

Choosing Your 'Tude

So, what kind of leader will you be? When you look behind you, will you see a crowd with smiles on their faces, or will you find yourself standing there all alone? IT ALL DEPENDS ON YOU. The more you weed out negative thoughts and replace them with positive ones, the more successful you will be as a leader. Remember—YOU'RE THE ONLY ONE WHO CAN CHOOSE YOUR 'TUDE!

"A POSITIVE ATTITUDE MAY NOT SOLVE ALL YOUR PROBLEMS, BUT IT WILL ANNOY ENOUGH PEOPLE TO MAKE IT WORTH THE EFFORT."

—HERM ALBRIGHT, ARTIST

9

From Dreams to Reality

Keep Looking Up

Are you ready to have an adventure? You're about to explore your vision and discover where it's taking you. On this step of the leadership ladder, you'll find that when it comes to dreaming, the best advice is **KEEP LOOKING UP!**

Walt Disney is a good example of a dreamer who kept looking up. Do

> **ALL GREAT LEADERS POSSESS TWO THINGS:**
> **THEY KNOW WHERE THEY'RE GOING, AND**
> **THEY CAN GET OTHERS TO FOLLOW THEM.**

you know many of his films are about making dreams come true? Even some of the songs from his films are about finding your dreams. Can you remember hearing Cinderella sing "A Dream Is a Wish Your Heart Makes"?

MR. ROGERS' NEIGHBORHOOD

Walt Disney knew where he wanted to take his dreams, and he persuaded others to follow him. So did Fred Rogers.

You may know him as Mr. Rogers. He's been on television for more than thirty years, and his show, Mr. Rogers' Neighborhood, *has touched the lives of millions of children.*

When he was a little boy, ministers were Fred's heroes. He wanted to be one when he grew up, but television sidetracked his plans. Fred saw television as an awesome way to reach kids, and he dreamed about making good television programs for young people. He knew he would be a minister someday, but he also knew his ministry would involve TV.

Mr. Rogers followed God's call. He held tight to his dream, and he shared it with others. He led a great team to create a wonderful television show—and he became a minister. Not only can Fred Rogers get his team to follow his vision, he gets young people to follow it, too. That's the mark of a great leader.

Or maybe, when you were little, you loved singing along with Jiminy Cricket when he sang, "When You Wish Upon a Star." Both of these songs reflect Walt Disney's vision to make his own dreams come true.

What You See Is What You Can Be

People don't follow a dream in itself. They follow the leader who has the dream and the ability to communicate it clearly. They usually accept the leader before they accept the dream.

Do you know people see dreams differently? The way they see them decides where they are on the leadership ladder.

Which one of these best describes you? Remember—you can always change the way you think and move to another step on the ladder.

Some people never see the dream.
(They are wanderers.)

Some people see it but never follow it on their own.
(They are followers.)

Some people see the dream and follow it.
(They are achievers.)

Some people see it, and follow it,
and help others see it. (They are leaders.)

A Locker Full of Wishes

Take a minute to write three wishes inside your locker notebook. They can be anything at all, so don't hold back! Have fun with this one.

We'll come back to your wishes later.

Dream Big Dreams

WHAT YOU SEE IS WHAT YOU GET

Think about how nice and refreshing it is to taste an ice-cold Coke. Hundreds of millions of people around the world have enjoyed this experience, thanks to the vision of Robert Woodruff. While he was president of Coca-Cola, during World War II, Woodruff boldly declared, "We will see that every man in uniform gets a bottle of Coca-Cola for five cents, wherever he is and what-ever the costs." When World War II ended, Woodruff said that before he died he wanted people all around the world to have tasted Coca-Cola. With careful planning and a lot of persistence, Woodruff and his team realized the dream. They reached their generation around the world for Coke.

Woodruff was a man of vision! He didn't just focus on getting by; he focused on winning big.

Ask yourself: "Is my dream going to make a difference in the world I live in?"

—*from Luis Palau's book* Dream Great Dreams

One day, the "Peanuts" characters Lucy and Linus had a wishbone, and they were going to pull it apart to make a wish. Lucy explained to Linus that if he got the bigger half of the wishbone his wish would come true. Linus said, "Do I have to say the wish out loud?" Lucy answered, "Of course you do. If you don't say it out loud it won't come true." So Lucy wished first. She said, "I wish for four new sweaters, a new bike, a new

pair of skates, a new dress, and one hundred dollars." Then it was time for Linus to wish. He said, "I wish for a long life for all of my friends, I wish for world peace, I wish for great advancements in medical research." When she heard that, Lucy took the wishbone and threw it in the garbage! "Linus," she said. "That's the trouble with you. You spoil everything."

Lucy wished small, and Linus wished big. Think about it. How big or little are your wishes?

Finding Your Vision

Maybe you're not sure where your vision is leading you. That's okay. Dreams don't grow all by themselves. You help them grow by looking around you. You can start by looking inside **yourself.**

There's No "I" in Others

When I was a teenager, my vision pretty much revolved around my own personal interests. My life centered on me. When I became a Christian, it seemed that the first radical change God performed in my life was with my vision. For the first time, my dreams changed. I began to focus on serving others. I wanted to help people, not just myself. My vision broadened.

Part of the transformation I owe to my father. While Christ was providing a new heart, I began to see the example of my dad in a new way. Jesus helped me on the inside, and my dad helped me on the outside, providing an external model for me. He was and is the most godly man I know. My vision began to imitate his vision—he was a pastor of a large church, so I wanted to be a pastor of a large church. My vision was literally shaped by Christ and my father.

Look inside You

☐ A person with a vision talks little but does much.

☐ A person with a vision finds strength from integrity.

☐ A person with a vision continues when problems arise.

Many celebrities have found their dreams in spite of obstacles. Singer/songwriter Carly Simon had a disability—she stuttered. Still, she became a great entertainer. Robin Williams has attention deficit hyperactivity disorder (ADHD). But that didn't stop him from becoming a

"WE HAVE GOT TO HAVE A DREAM, IF WE ARE GOING TO MAKE A DREAM COME TRUE."

—DENIS WAITLEY, PSYCHOLOGIST

great actor and comedian. Athlete Bruce Jenner is dyslexic. And he went on to become a U.S. Olympic gold medalist.

TRUE LEADERS KEEP FOLLOWING THEIR DREAMS—*no matter what happens.* So take a look inside. Are you letting something stop you from dreaming big dreams?

Look behind You

A vision should be greater than the person who has it. Successful leaders will tell you they don't know everything. They're always looking for people who can help make their dreams come true. What would Helen Keller have been without her teacher Anne Sullivan? Or what would Wynona Judd be without the influence of her mother, Naomi? Or Samson without Delilah?

Can you think of some other great partnerships? History is filled with them. How about Ben and Jerry—the ice-cream guys!

BEN AND JERRY

Ben and Jerry met in junior high school, and years later they went into the ice cream business together. Ben was the inventive one on the team, creative and unpredictable. When he was a kid, he created his own favorite flavors by mushing candy and cookies into his ice cream. Jerry was the educated one. He graduated from high school with a National Merit Scholarship, and he went on to earn a four-year business degree. The men sold their first scoops of ice cream in a small remodeled gas station in Vermont. The rest is history. Ben and Jerry, working together, built their dream into a multimillion-dollar business.

Would we have great flavor names like **PHiSH FOOD** and **CHUNKY MONKEY** if it weren't for Ben? Maybe not. Would Ben and Jerry's have grown to be so big had it not been for Jerry? I doubt it. Great things happen when a team is formed. Like the old saying goes, "Two heads are better than one."

Think of some people who can help make your dreams come true.

Look around You:
What's Happening to Others?

A little boy went to his first orchestra concert. He thought the huge auditorium, the people in their dressy clothes, and the big sound of the orchestra were totally awesome. Of all the instruments he heard, he liked the cymbals best. That first loud crash echoing through his body felt so cool! He noticed, though, that most of the time the cymbal guy just stood there while the other musicians played. Only a few times did the cymbal guy get to make a big crash.

After the concert, the little boy's parents took him backstage to meet the musicians. The boy hurried over to the cymbal player. "Hey, mister," he said, "how much do you need to know to play the cymbals?" The cymbal player thought for a while and then answered, "You don't have to know much at all. You only have to know when."

Knowing *when* is a really important part of sharing your dream. A GOOD IDEA BECOMES GREAT WHEN THE PEOPLE ARE READY FOR THE IDEA. If you run too far ahead, you lose your power to influence others. And without influence, your dream will fall flat on its face.

Think about it: Are you a patient person, or do you like to run on ahead?

Look above You: What Does God Expect of You?

God's gift to you is your *potential*—in other words, your talents and abilities. Your gift back to God is what you do with your potential. Great leaders sense a "higher calling," one that lifts them above themselves. That's what happened to Mr. Rogers. He felt God tugging at him and leading him toward a career in television.

Take time to pray about your dreams. Ask God to show you where He wants you to go and what He wants you to do.

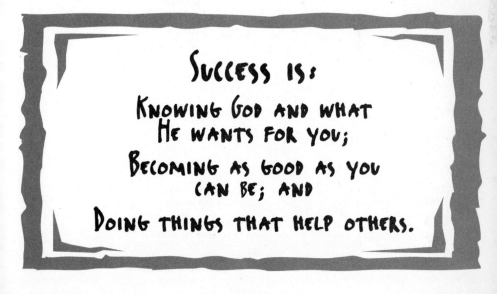

SUCCESS IS:
KNOWING GOD AND WHAT HE WANTS FOR YOU;
BECOMING AS GOOD AS YOU CAN BE; AND
DOING THINGS THAT HELP OTHERS.

A Locker Full of Visions

What do you *really* want to do? How will your vision make a difference?

Now, check this out. If you had anything you wanted—unlimited time, unlimited money, unlimited information, and all the help you could ask for—**what would you do?** Think about it. Fill in the blanks from the locker below in your locker notebook, then write about your vision .

Is your vision different from any of the wishes you wrote in your notebook about the locker on page 9?

Getting Others to Share Your Dream

"All men dream: but not equally. Those who dream by night in the dusty recesses of their minds wake in the day to find that it was vanity: but the dreamers of the day are dangerous men, for they may act their dream with open eyes, to make it possible."

—*T. E. Lawrence, British soldier and writer (also known as Lawrence of Arabia)*

You See What You Are Prepared to See

For a vision to grow and create a following, a leader has to influence others to follow. That can be hard sometimes, because PEOPLE SEE THINGS DIFFERENTLY.

Jesus and the Blind Man

The tenth chapter of Mark tells the story of Bartimaeus, a blind beggar who was sitting by the side of the road. (Begging was about all a blind person could do in those days.) When Bartimaeus heard Jesus was walking by, he kept calling out to Him, "Have mercy on me. Have mercy on me." Jesus' followers tried to quiet him down, but the harder they tried, the louder he became. "Jesus, have mercy on me!" he yelled—until Jesus heard him.

The people in the crowd meant well. Those who were trying to make Bartimaeus shut up may have given him food or a little money. They could accept him as a beggar, but not as an equal.

But Jesus saw things differently. He saw that He could make a difference in the life of one man, so He stopped everything and told the people to tell Bartimaeus to come to Him. Jesus could have said, "Give him some money or food to settle him down." But He didn't. Jesus understood that Bartimaeus wanted to be one of the followers—he wanted to be included. Jesus listened to the blind man, and He healed him.

Does Bartimaeus Live Near You?

This same thing happens today. Some people see beggars on the street and walk right by. Other people see beggars on the street and create a vision to help them. What's up with that? Why is it that two people can be in the same place at the same time and both see entirely different things? It's simple. We see what we are prepared to see—*not what is*. An awesome leader understands this and asks three things:

- [ ] What do others see?
- [ ] Why do they see it that way?
- [ ] How can I change the way they see it?

Create a Masterpiece

Great leaders explain their vision by "painting a picture" for their followers. Every great vision has certain ingredients, and a great leader makes the people understand, appreciate, and "see" them.

You'll need the following to create your masterpiece:

HORIZON

Where you put the horizon shows people how big the dream can be. Each person will decide how high in the sky he or she wants to go. Your responsibility, as the leader, is to put plenty of sky into the picture. You want to encourage your followers to **reach for the stars!**

Helen and Anne

Anne Sullivan, Helen Keller's teacher, was a leader who put a lot of sky into the picture. She encouraged Helen, who was deaf and blind and could not speak, to dream big. Young Helen learned to read and write and even speak, and she graduated from college. She dedicated her life to improving conditions for deaf and blind people all over the world. Could Helen have done it without a leader like Anne?

SUN

The sun in your picture brings warmth and hope. **Light brings out good things in people.** If you want to be a great leader, it's up to you to bring light to your team and to keep hope alive.

Think about how a warm, sunny day feels compared to a cold, rainy one. Do you feel happier when the sun shines? Most people do. It's the same way when you compare a strong leader with a weak one. A strong and sunny leader makes things seem fun and worth doing. A weak and cold leader makes a project a total yawn.

MOUNTAINS

Every vision has its challenges. Your job is to convince people to "climb the mountains and scale the walls."

Joni Eareckson Tada

When she was a teenager, Joni Eareckson Tada was paralyzed from the neck down in a diving accident. Today her artwork (done by holding a brush in her teeth) is on greeting cards, posters, and stationery. Joni has a daily radio broadcast, she wrote the story of her life in a book called Joni, *and when that book was turned into a movie she played herself. Above all her other accomplishments, Joni is a great leader. She convinces people to "climb the mountains and scale the walls!"*

BIRDS

Birds in your picture represent two more things you want your followers to have—freedom and spirit. Imagine watching an eagle glide effortlessly toward the mountains. Does that make your spirit **SOAR** and give you a sense of **FREEDOM?** That's how you want others to feel when they "see" your dream.

> "HOLD FAST TO DREAMS, FOR IF DREAMS DIE, LIFE IS A BROKEN-WINGED BIRD THAT CANNOT FLY."
>
> —LANGSTON HUGHES, POET

FLOWERS

Even when you're doing something you totally love, you have to take a break sometimes. The journey toward finding any great dream takes time. Make sure the scenery in your painting includes rest stops along the way—places to "smell flowers" and get refreshed. It's okay to play sometimes. Stop once in a while to have a soda and hang with your friends.

PATH

Your dream needs a place to begin and a path to follow. It's your job to lead the way.

A traveler through a rugged country asked his Indian guide, "How can you pick your way over these jagged peaks and dangerous trails without ever losing your way?" The guide answered, "I have near and far vision. With one I see what is directly ahead of me; with the other I guide my course by the stars."

YOURSELF

Don't forget to put yourself in the picture! This will show you think your dream is cool and that you're an important part of the team. Remember—your followers need a model to follow—and that model is *y-o-u.*

PUT THE THINGS THEY LOVE IN THE PICTURE

Before you're through, put what's important to your followers in your picture. Listen to what your team members have to say. GREAT LEADERS DON'T WORK ALONE. They work with their team to accomplish great things. Think about how the dreams you share will make all of your lives better.

Your Best Friend's Locker

Imagine you want your best friend to "see" your vision. Which things will you put in your "painting" that will motivate your friend to share your dream? Describe them in your locker notebook.

My vision:
To feed
hungry
children.

My Best Friend

I'd put
these things
in my
painting:

My friend
and I
working
together

Lots of
little kids

Get These Dudes Out of My Dream!

There are ten kinds of people who can get in the way of your dream becoming a reality. I call them the Dream Blockers. Watch out for these dudes. And make sure you're not one of them!

1. Limited Leaders

Limited Leaders can't see the dream and can't pass it on.

Warren heard his parents talking about a new soup kitchen in the community, so he decided he'd like to collect canned food to help the kitchen get started. He asked everyone in his Sunday school class to donate a can

> "I ALWAYS HAVE TO DREAM UP THERE AGAINST THE STARS. IF I DON'T DREAM I WILL MAKE IT, I WON'T EVEN GET CLOSE."
>
> —HENRY J. KAISER,
> INDUSTRIALIST

of food next Sunday. They did, but still, Warren was able to collect only fifteen cans of food—not much when you're trying to feed several dozen, or maybe hundreds, of people every day. How much more food could Warren have collected if he'd asked everyone in his church to donate food? Or everyone in his school? Or everyone in his neighborhood?

This shows what a Limited Leader will do. Warren couldn't see the dream of feeding so many people every day, so he didn't let his vision of how he could help go beyond his small circle of friends in Sunday school.

2. Concrete Thinkers

Concrete Thinkers have their feet stuck in the goo. They can't see beyond the moment.

Charlie Brown, a **CREATIVE** Thinker, holds up his hands for Lucy to see. He says, "These are hands which may some day accomplish great things. These are hands which may some day do marvelous works! They may build mighty bridges, or heal the sick, or hit home runs, or write soul-stirring novels! These are hands which may some day change the course of destiny!" Lucy, a **CONCRETE** Thinker, who always sees things as they are, replies, "They've got jelly on them."

Are you Lucy or Charlie Brown? A Creative Thinker or a Concrete Thinker?

3. DOGMATIC TALKERS

Dogmatic Talkers are Dream Blockers. To be absolutely certain about something, you either have to know everything or nothing about it. Most of the time, a Dogmatic Talker knows nothing, but says something anyway.

Think about Warren again. If he were a Dogmatic Talker, he might say, "They don't need that much food, I'm sure. A soup kitchen probably gets donations from lots of groups. They don't depend on just me. Maybe I shouldn't even take these few cans."

What do you think? Does Warren know what he's talking about? Should he ask the soup kitchen director how much food it takes to run a soup kitchen or if enough donations are coming in to support it?

4. BIG-TIME LOSERS

Big-Time Losers look at past failures and fear the risk of going after a dream. Their motto is: "If at first you don't succeed, destroy any evidence that you've tried." They may also try to destroy everyone's attempt to try again.

When Becky was in the choir, she tried to get a group together to entertain residents at a local nursing home. Nobody was interested. *It was a dumb idea,* Becky thought. The next year, one of Becky's classmates had the same idea, but for a local hospital. "It's a dumb idea," Becky said.

Why do you think Becky said that? Big-Time Losers don't have a lot of self-confidence. Becky might have been so afraid of failing again that she wanted no part in even trying.

5. Satisfied Sitters

Satisfied Sitters like comfort, predictability, and security in life. Sometimes that leads to laziness, boredom, and no vision.

A nest is a good place for a robin while it's in an egg. But it's a bad place for a robin when it has wings. It's a good place to be hatched in, but it's a poor place to fly in.

It's always sad when people don't want to leave the nests of their lives.

6. Stuck-in-a-Rut'ers

Stuck-in-a-Rut'ers do things the same way just because that's how they've always done them. They're stuck in the past, and they can't move on.

Several months went by at the soup kitchen, and each month, Warren donated a few cans of food from his Sunday school. One day, the director of the soup kitchen asked Warren if he would lead a campaign in his school to gather volunteers to work in the kitchen over the Christmas holidays.

Warren said, "But my friends and I have been donating food. That's what we do."

The director told him the community had donated plenty of food to get through the holidays, but she said many of her volunteers would be out of town for Christmas, and she didn't know how she could serve the expected two hundred hungry people without more help.

"But we've never done that!" Warren said. "We just donate food!"

Do you know any Stuck-in-a-Rut'ers?

7. Follow the Leaders

Follow the Leaders want to be a part of, not apart from, the group. And they will grab the dream only after most of the other followers do. Don't look for these guys at the front of the line.

The youth director at church had tried for two years, since he came to the church, to get the youth group to raise money to go on a mission trip. But no one seemed interested. Then one day, Yvette joined the church with her family. Full of enthusiasm and dedicated to following Jesus, Yvette thought the idea of a mission trip was fabulous and told the youth director she'd love to go and asked him how she could help raise money. After that, one by one, the other kids in the group decided they wanted to help with the trip, too.

Follow the Leaders like to play things **SAFE**. They want to make sure that something will work before they get on board.

8. Problem Seers

Problem Seers see only problems.

Warren found an excuse for why he shouldn't find some fellow students to volunteer at the soup kitchen. "We could get hurt," he told the director. "You never know what might happen. Someone could spill a pot of soup on himself. Or we could hurt someone. . . ."

Problem Seers will throw an obstacle into even the greatest dream. Watch out!

9. Self-Seekers.

Self-Seekers are vision-busters. They think only of me-me-me.

Warren behaved like a Self-Seeker when he didn't want to volunteer to serve food at the soup kitchen. When he thought of having to get up early on Christmas morning, missing the family celebration, then standing in a serving line to feed people he didn't know, all he could think of was how much he wanted to stay home and not get involved. Surely someone would volunteer if he and his friends didn't.

Great dreams are fulfilled when everyone works for a common goal.

10. FAILURE FORECASTERS

Failure Forecasters spray pessimism everywhere they go. Shadows rule all their pictures. Their outlook is gloomy. They say stuff like: "It doesn't matter if the cup is half full or half empty. Whatever's inside is evaporating anyway."

Failure Forecasters are like the man who gathered with many others at the Hudson River to see the first steamship launched. He kept saying, "They'll never get her going. They'll never get her going." But they did. The steamship belched and moved out fast. Immediately, the

It's hard to hit goals you can't see.

same man said, "They'll never get her stopped. They'll never get her stopped." But they did. Then the man paused and said, "They'll never get her back."

Do you know a Failure Forecaster?

Keep Your Dream Going

Do you have a clear idea of what your vision is and where it's taking you? Do you know how to *keep your dream alive?* Doing that is the most important thing of all.

In your locker notebook, make a list of dreamers—those who had an idea and kept their dream alive. These can be people you know, celebrities, historical figures. When you work at realizing your own dreams, remember them.

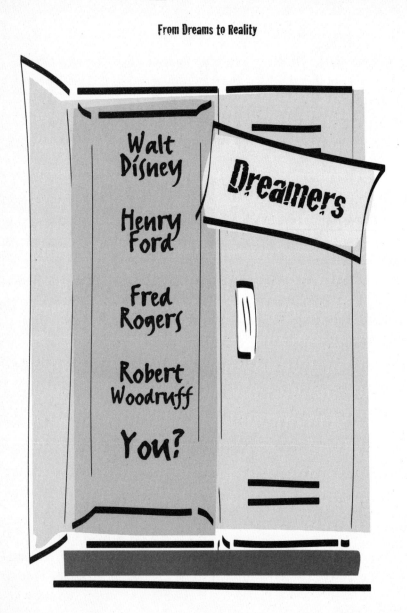

10
Your Turn to Lead

Great leaders help others to realize their dreams.

We Were Made for One Another

By now your locker notebook is stuffed with cool things such as influence, integrity, change, priorities, problem-solving, willpower, and attitude. And you've probably thrown some dreams in there, too. You've filled the lockers with the knowledge that will make you into an awesome leader. So what do you do now? **Lead!**

To lead, you have to have followers, right? So, let's talk about *them* for a change. After all—we were made for one another! God created us to work as a team.

How far you go with your dreams depends on what kind of relationships you develop. Great leaders don't want to do things all by themselves or get all the credit. Instead, they rely on others to help them get the job done.

Ron Howard

Ron Howard began his career as a child actor. You might remember him as Opie on The Andy Griffith Show *or Richie on* Happy Days. *The more Ron was around cameras and sets, the more he dreamed of becoming a movie director. Today, he is one of the most well-known and well-respected directors in Hollywood. His pictures include* Apollo 13, Backdraft, *and* How the Grinch Stole Christmas.

Ron is a success not only because he has the vision to turn good scripts into great movies, but also because he's awesome at forming good relationships. He knows how to put together a dream team of actors, set designers, makeup artists, and special effects wizards. Ron understands he can't make movies all by himself. His job, as a leader, is to get others to share his vision. Ron does a great job of leading. He not only inspires his followers to share his dreams and to do a good job, but he also knows how to get along with people— and that's what keeps his dreams alive.

The better you get along with people, the greater the chance of realizing your dreams.

We Sail the Sea of Humanity in Relation Ships

My earliest relationship lessons came from my dad. I was a young teenager when I started to notice his masterful people skills. When we went to summer camp meetings, I would watch him talk with others and encourage them. He would walk slowly through the crowds, lifting everyone's spirits. Once I timed him as he strolled across the yard in front of the dining hall. I was in a hurry to get to the pool. It took him forty-five minutes to take a five-minute walk—because he would stop and make everyone feel like the most important person in the world. It was then that I went from frustration to admiration for him. My impatience gave way as I saw what his patience did for others.

I wanted so much to learn those same skills that I approached him, as a teenager, and asked if he would put me through a Dale Carnegie course on relationship skills. He not only did, but also went through it with me—as if he needed to improve! It was during these days that I learned that making people feel special really motivates them.

> "I SUPPOSE LEADERSHIP AT ONE TIME MEANT MUSCLES, BUT TODAY IT MEANS GETTING ALONG WITH PEOPLE."
>
> —INDIRA GANDHI,
> FORMER PRIME MINISTER
> OF INDIA

It's Not What You Think!

Amaya hardly ever speaks to anyone. Most people think she's "stuck-up." Do you know someone like Amaya? Do you *really* know that person? Maybe that person is just quiet and shy and has trouble making friends. **FIRST IMPRESSIONS AREN'T ALWAYS WHAT THEY SEEM.**

We often make the wrong assumptions about people. If you assume a person won't be a good friend, then that's the way you'll treat her. If you assume a person has a lot to give a friendship, you'll probably treat that person in a more positive way.

Check out these assumptions. If you remember them, you'll make lots of friends.

ASSUMPTION 1

Everyone Wants to Be Valued

People need to feel **IMPORTANT!** It's a leader's job to make people feel valued.

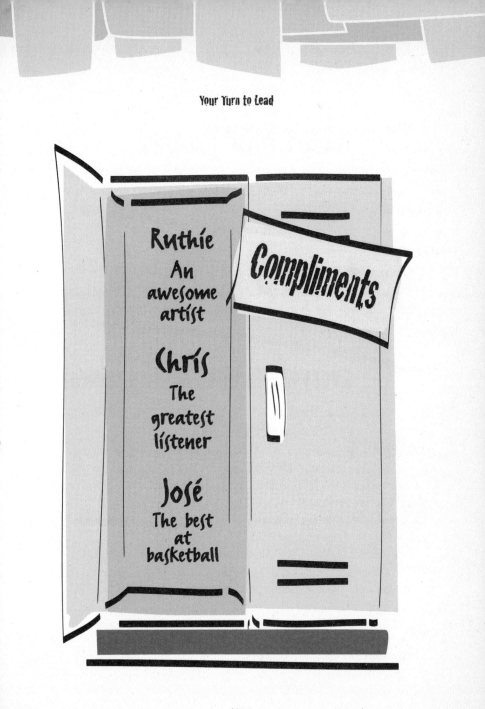

A Locker Filled with Compliments

In your locker notebook, write down the names of three of your friends. Below each name, write a compliment that is sure to boost his or her self-esteem. Remember to share the compliments the next time you see your friends.

ASSUMPTION 2

Everyone Needs Encouragement

Ming Lee

Ming Lee works part-time as a dance instructor. She was getting a group of elementary school girls ready for a competition when she noticed that one of the little girls wasn't dancing as well as she usually danced. Ming Lee worried that something might be wrong.

"Monica," Ming Lee said when they were alone, "you don't seem to be your-self. Is something bothering you?"

"I'm worried about the contest," Monica answered. "What if I mess up and we lose?"

"If that happens," Ming Lee said, "it won't be the end of the world. You're a great dancer, and all I ask is that you try to do your best."

Ming Lee is an encouraging leader. Encouragement is like oxygen for the soul. Henry Ford said, "My best friend is the one who brings out the best in me." Every leader wants to bring out the best in people. And every successful leader knows encouragement is the way to do it.

Think about the people who encourage you when things aren't going well. Those people are your true friends. And what about you? *Are you an encourager?* The Bible says in Hebrews 3:13: "Encourage each other every day."

A Locker Filled with Encouragement

This leadership locker is filled with encouraging words. Can you think of others?

"Hang in there."

"I'm proud of you."

"I know you can do it."

"Jesus loves you."

"You're doing great."

"Can I help?"

"Do you want to talk about it?"

Encouragement

ASSUMPTION 3

Everyone Needs a Role Model

VINCE LOMBARDI

Vince Lombardi was one of the greatest football coaches in history. He led the Green Bay Packers to five NFL Championships and two Super Bowls. How did he do it? By knowing how to get the best out of his players.

Lombardi focused on teamwork. He knew a leader must support his team first, before anything else. He understood that if you treat people with respect and treat them like winners, they'll perform like winners. He demanded dedication and sacrifice from every player, and at the same time, he made every player feel he was a part of the team. At least one of his players described Lombardi as "the fairest man I've ever met."

Coach Lombardi's success is a great example of how people respond to someone who is a good role model.

It's Your Turn to Lead

You've learned a lot about being a good role model. Now, it's up to you to show your friends what you've learned. You know that success doesn't happen overnight and that it doesn't happen by sitting still. It's about all those steps on the leadership ladder—influence, integrity, change, priorities, problem-solving, willpower, and attitude. PASS IT ON! Teach your friends

Always tell the truth.

Encourage teamwork.

Have a sense of humor.

Role Model

by setting a good example and by always being a good role model. The better role model you are, the more successful your relationships will be.

In your leadership notebook, list three ways you can be a good role model for your friends.

People Want to Participate

When Sam's church offered a computer class on building Web pages, Sam couldn't wait to sign up. He thought it would be cool to have his own home page where he could share his ideas with family and friends. But the class wasn't at all what Sam expected.

The teacher was unprepared. She read instructions from a book, and instead of letting the students participate, she showed them what to do on one computer that was set up at the front of the room. Twenty-six people showed up for class the first week. By the second week, there were only ten.

A bad teacher can make even the most interesting subject boring. It's the same way with dreams. You can have the coolest vision in the world, and watch it fall flat on its face. Why? Because you didn't know how to motivate people. We all want things to be interesting and fun, and we want to feel like we own a part of the action.

When you are a leader, **motivation**—or making others want to participate—is totally your job. When you lead a group of people, it's up to you to jump-start the team.

The Five Biggest Motivational Turnons

1. PEOPLE WANT TO BELIEVE THEIR CONTRIBUTIONS ARE VALUABLE.

2. PEOPLE WANT TO BE A PART OF DREAM-MAKING AND PLANNING.

3. PEOPLE WANT RECOGNITION. (THIS IS A BIGGIE.)

4. PEOPLE WANT CLEAR IDEAS OF WHAT THEY ARE EXPECTED TO DO.

5. PEOPLE WANT TO KNOW THEY CAN BE SUCCESSFUL.

Team members want certain things, and a good leader will work with them to help them get those things.

If you remember to give your followers these five things, your team will take off running. If you forget to do these things, they'll be snoozing.

The Four Biggest Motivational Turnoffs

1. Jack Be-Little

Jack was leading a youth group meeting at his church. The group was discussing themes for a Valentine's Day party, and the discussion got out of hand. Everyone was silly that night, and there was a lot of laughing and funny comments. In the middle of all the joking, Martin, one of the quieter boys in the group, offered a suggestion for a theme. Without thinking, Jack said, "Martin, you're such a dork!" He meant it in fun, but he could tell by looking at Martin's red face that he was embarrassed.

Martin wasn't one who spoke up often, and Jack's remarks sure didn't motivate him to speak up again.

> "Keep away from people who try to belittle your ambitions. Small people always do that, but the really great make you feel that you, too, can become great."
>
> —Mark Twain, author

Cutting remarks, even in jest, can hurt. A good leader knows to be **sensitive,** even when having fun.

2. THE MANIPULATOR

Tonika didn't like being the record keeper for her Spanish club. All a record keeper does is write, write, write. So Tonika tried to persuade her classmate, Marcie, to take the job.

But instead of being honest, Tonika was manipulative. "Hey, Marcie," she said. "How would you like to be record keeper for Spanish club? It's such a **totally cool** thing to do."

What do you think of what Tonika did? Guess what Marcie thought. She saw right through Tonika. Marcie knew the job was a drag, and there was no way she would help Tonika out—especially since she had tried to trick Marcie into taking the job.

Manipulators always have some sort of sneaky plan in mind. WATCH OUT! If there's something they don't want to do, they'll try to get you to do it. Or if there's some way you can help them, they'll suddenly be your best friend. Manipulators do things for the good of themselves and not for the good of the team.

No one likes to feel manipulated or used. Manipulation, no matter how slight, tears down the walls of TRUST in a relationship. A leader gains more by being honest and real than by being sneaky. If you build up people through encouragement and praise, then they'll be motivated and loyal. Remember—GIVE AND IT SHALL BE GIVEN TO YOU.

3. The Fuzz Buster

Have you heard of "warm fuzzies"? They're words or acts of encouragement or comfort. Everyone needs warm fuzzies—in other words, everyone needs other people to be sensitive to their feelings. We all need to feel we're important and cared about.

Tai was a good team leader, but she had a habit of getting buried in her work. If someone asked her a question while she was working, she kept on doing what she was doing. She answered the question, but she never looked up, and she never seemed interested in what the other person had to say. Soon, she got the reputation of being a snob, and people weren't motivated to follow her.

Without meaning to be, Tai was a Fuzz Buster. She missed opportunities to give her team warm fuzzies. Great leaders make people their priority. They never appear preoccupied or in a hurry. One of the best ways not to be a Fuzz Buster is to learn to be a good and caring listener. Remember— put people first!

> "It takes a great man to be a good listener."
>
> —Calvin Coolidge, thirtieth president of the United States

4. The Squasher

Squashers don't care about growing a team. They don't encourage team members to stretch and try new things. After a while, the dream gets stale. People aren't motivated to follow Squashers, so eventually they go away and find new dreams to chase. Squashers don't build team spirit; they tear it down.

QUENTIN

Quentin and Naomi were part of a brass quartet that was scheduled to represent their school band in the upcoming district solo and ensemble contest. They were both excellent players—Quentin played first-chair trumpet, and Naomi played first-chair trombone. The only problem was that the other two players in the quartet—Gabe and Ingrid—weren't very good.

Their school was small, and by the time Quentin got around to forming his quartet, all the other good players except Naomi had joined other ensembles. Gabe and Ingrid, though, were excited to be in the quartet with Quentin and Naomi.

All the other ensembles were busy most afternoons after school, practicing for the contest, but Quentin's quartet practiced only once a week, and for only half an hour. One afternoon after a particularly bad rehearsal, Naomi talked to Quentin about needing more practice. He shrugged. "Why bother?" he said. "We're terrible." Gabe and Ingrid, who were still sitting there, both lowered their heads.

Quentin was a Squasher. Instead of encouraging Gabe and Ingrid and joining Naomi to help them learn to be better players, he squashed their hopes of ever being a winning quartet. Could they have won? Maybe, if they'd practiced and encouraged one another.

If you want to be a great leader, give your team members opportunities to **TRY NEW THINGS** and learn new skills. Don't feel threatened by the achievements of others; instead, be supportive of their successes.

What's in It for Me?

How many times have you stopped doing something because you weren't getting anything out of it? Maybe it was music lessons, or

MATT HATES MATH

Matt had good grades in school, except for one subject: math. He had a mental block when it came to numbers. They made him sweat. Yet Matt's favorite thing in the world was baseball. He played shortstop, and he was one of the best players on his team. But because he failed math during the last grading period, school rules said he couldn't play baseball until his grade came up.

While Matt was out, the coach moved Lamar, who normally played a great outfield, in to shortstop. But Lamar didn't like playing shortstop because that wasn't his best position, and as the season wore on, he was getting more and more frustrated with the pressure of having to play a position he wasn't very good at. He was losing his concentration on the field, and he knew he was not contributing much to the team anymore. He began to consider quitting.

The team pitcher, Everett, found out about Lamar's frustration, and he knew the team didn't need to lose two good players in one season. Then he remembered something special he knew about Lamar, and he got an idea. Everett knew Lamar was a whiz in math. In fact, he was so good with numbers that he was also on the school's math team. Everett talked to the coach, then his two teammates, and proposed a plan: Three afternoons a week, Lamar would tutor Matt in math. Soon, Matt's grades came up, and he got to return to the team—and to shortstop. That meant Lamar could go back to the outfield he loved. Matt was finally able to understand all those numbers in math, and Lamar received the satisfaction of knowing he had helped a teammate gain some valuable knowledge.

sports, or a club. We all have different wants and needs, and sometimes when we try something new, we find that it just doesn't fit. Then what happens?

Everyone wants to know his contribution is making a difference. You can help with that by really knowing each person on your team.

What things are they good at?
What things aren't they good at?

People get bored and frustrated when they are assigned tasks in their weak areas. Doing things they enjoy motivates them.

Can You Confront?

Nobody likes to face CONFLICT, but conflict is a part of relationships. Conflict left unresolved will stop your team cold. When members of your team are the root of a problem, it's your job as a leader to confront them. That's hard for most leaders to do, but a great leader does it and does it well. If just reading the word CONFRONT makes you break out in hives, try using the words CLEAR UP instead. Think of resolving conflict as clearing up issues instead of confronting people.

Use these Ten Commandments of Clearing Up whenever you have an issue to resolve. They will help you get your relationships back on track.

Ten Commandments of Clearing Up

1. Do it privately, not publicly.

2. Do it as soon as possible. That's better than waiting until things get worse.

3. Deal with one issue at a time. Don't overload the person with a long list of issues.

4. Once you've made a point, don't keep repeating it.

5. Deal only with actions the person can change. If you ask someone to do something that person is unable to do, frustration builds up in your relationship.

6. Avoid sarcasm. Sarcasm signals you are angry at PEOPLE, not at their actions. It may cause them to resent you.

7. Avoid words like ALWAYS and NEVER. They usually make people defensive.

8. Present criticisms as suggestions or questions, if possible.

9. Don't apologize for confronting the person. It may send the message that you aren't sure you had the right to say what you did.

10. Don't forget the compliments! Use what I call the "sandwich" approach: Compliment-Confront-Compliment.

What Did You Say?

Good relationships are built on good listening. A good leader listens to people with more than ears and hears more than words. Take this quiz to see what kind of listener you are. Across the top of a page in your locker notebook, write these words: **Always, Usually, Almost Never, Never.** Then draw a line between each phrase, going from the top of the page toward the bottom. This should give you four columns in which to mark your

THE LISTENING QUIZ

1. When someone is speaking, how often do you interrupt before he or she finishes?

2. How often do you try to understand what a speaker is feeling?

3. When a teacher is speaking and you're taking notes, how often do you write down key facts and phrases?

4. If you're not sure what a teacher or speaker meant, do you ask that person to explain?

5. How often do you feel angry or upset when you disagree with a teacher or speaker?

6. How often do you tune out distractions when listening?

7. Do you try to act interested in what someone is saying, even when you're not?

answers. Then down the left side of the page, number seven lines. As you take the quiz, place a check in your notebook under the column that answers these questions about you.

Scoring: Give yourself four points if the answer to a question is *Always*; three points for *Usually*; two for *Almost Never*; and one for *Never*.

26 or higher:	Excellent! You're an awesome listener.
22-25:	Good. You are a better-than-average listener.
18-21:	You need to spend more time learning to listen.
17 or lower:	You really need to work on your listening skills.

What most people want is to be listened to, respected, and understood. The minute people see they are being understood, they become more motivated to understand *your* point of view. So, if you want great relationships—**LEARN TO BE A GREAT LISTENER.**

Good friends bonding.

Are You Getting What You Give?

When relationships are out of balance, problems occur. Think of someone with whom you don't always get along. In your locker notebook, list what you get from the relationship. Then list what you give to the relationship.

Now compare the two lists. Don't count the number of items. Instead, ask yourself: "Comparing what I give to what I get, who is getting the better deal?"

What can you do to improve the relationship? When two people get an equally good deal, they **RESPECT** one another. Look at the examples in the lockers on page 210. Who do you think is getting the better deal?

Don't Steal Their Ego Food!

"EGO FOOD" is what people need to build their self-esteem. Good leaders don't steal it. For example, if a person says, "I've got a lot of homework to do," and you reply, "*You've* got a lot of homework! You should see how much homework *I've* got," you've stolen their ego food. It's like you're saying, "You think you've got it bad? Well, don't complain to me, because I've got it worse."

Stealing someone's ego food is an easy thing to do. Just for fun, tomorrow see how many times you catch yourself satisfying your own self-esteem needs by stealing away someone else's ego food.

GOOD RELATIONSHIPS GROW FROM BOOSTING SELF-ESTEEM, so be careful that you don't take more than you give.

What I Get

Sue . . .
always shows
up on time,
is willing to
help me when I
really need it,
lets me borrow
her tennis
racket.

What I Give

I . . .
help Sue with
her homework,
listen to her
problems,
hang out with
her—even when
I have other
stuff to do.

Climb to the Top of the Ladder

That's it. You've done it! You've reached the top of the leadership ladder, and you're a true leader. How cool is that? You've learned that "leader" is more than just a title. It's who you are and how you choose to live your life. It's setting a good example, reaching for your dreams, and having awesome relationships. Now all you have to do is practice what you've learned. Practice your leadership skills every day. The more you practice, the better leader you'll be. And remember—*you're leading from the lockers.* Whenever you get stuck, you can pull out your locker notebook and find it stuffed with all sorts of great leadership tips. So do it! Go out there and lead!

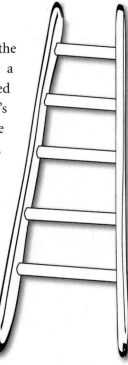

Listen to people.

Be with them.

Love them.

Start with what they know.

Build on what they have.

And of the best leaders,

When their job is through,

And their work is done,

The People will say,

"We did it together!"

—Based on an old Chinese poem